A Glossary for Archivists, Manuscript Curators, and Records Managers

compiled by
Lewis J. Bellardo
and Lynn Lady Bellardo

The Society of American Archivists

Chicago

1992

♾ *A Glossary for Archivists, Manuscript Curators, and Records Managers* is printed on alkaline, acid-free printing paper manufactured with no groundwood pulp. As such, it substantially meets the requirements of the American National Standards Institute—Permanence of Paper for Printed Library Materials, ANSI 239.48-1984. Typesetting and printing of this publication is done by Port City Press of Baltimore, Maryland. Manufactured in the United States.

ISBN 0-931828-79-1

TABLE OF CONTENTS

Dedication

This glossary is dedicated to the memory of Kenneth Munden, a longtime member of the Society of American Archivists and editor of its journal, the *American Archivist,* from 1960 to 1968. The publication of this glossary has been partially supported through a generous gift from his wife, Lia Munden.

Preface

The seven new titles in SAA's Archival Fundamentals Series have been conceived and written to be a foundation for modern archival theory and practice. Like the previous Basic Manual Series that for more than a dozen years excelled in articulating and advancing archival knowledge and skills, they are intended for a *general* audience within the archival profession and to have widespread application. They will strengthen and augment the knowledge and skills of archivists, general practitioners, and specialists alike, who are performing a wide range of archival duties in all types of archival and manuscript repositories.

This series is designed to encompass the basic archival functions enumerated by SAA's Guidelines for Graduate Archival Education. The volumes discuss the theoretical principles that underlie archival practice, the functions and activities that are common within the archival profession, and the techniques that represent the best of current practice. They give practical advice, enabling today's practitioners to prepare for the challenges of rapid change within the archival profession.

Together with more specialized manuals also available from SAA, the Archival Fundamentals Series should form the core of any archivist's working library. The series has particular value for newcomers to the profession, including students, who wish to have a broad overview of archival work and an in-depth treatment of its major components. The volumes in the series will also serve as invaluable guides and reference works for more experienced archivists, especially in working with new staff members, volunteers, and others. It is our hope that the Archival Fundamentals Series will be a benchmark in the archival literature for many years to come.

Preparing these publications has been a collaborative effort. The authors have contributed the most, of course, but SAA readers, reviewers, staff members, and Editorial Board members have assisted greatly. I would particularly like to thank Donn Neal, Tim Ericson, and Anne Diffendal, Executive Directors; Susan Grigg, Chair of the Editorial Board, whose good counsel and support never failed; and Teresa Brinati, Managing Editor, who brought the volumes from text to publication.

In addition, the Society expresses its deep appreciation to the National Historical Publications and Records Commission, which funded the preparation and initial printing of the series.

Mary Jo Pugh, Editor
Archival Fundamentals Series

Acknowledgments

The most enjoyable part of any project of this kind is the opportunity to thank those whose assistance made it all possible. We enthusiastically seize this opportunity to acknowledge the following colleagues and friends. In so doing, we accept sole responsibility for any deficiencies in the volume.

First, we thank all the members of the SAA Glossary Advisory Committee who suggested terms, provided definitions, supplied written and oral advice and critiques, who edited our work, and who were a great source of moral support. The committee members are: Nicholas C. Burckel, Paul Conway, Virginia Daley, Luciana Duranti, Frank B. Evans, Judith Fortson, David B. Gracy II, David E. Horn, Harold Naugler, Roy H. Tryon, and Lisa B. Weber. Each provided invaluable assistance.

In a very real sense Frank Evans is the father of this project. He was a driving force in the preparation of the first SAA glossary and also served with distinction on the international committee that produced the International Council on Archives' *Dictionary of Archival Terminology*. More than this, throughout his long and distinguished career he has served as a teacher of terminology to an entire generation of archivists. Throughout this project, he was an advisor, critic, and friend.

Two other committee members invested enormous amounts of time and energy in the project. Luciana Duranti prepared drafts of numerous terms, added many important concepts to the glossary, and introduced the authors to the field of diplomatics. Lisa Weber provided valuable insights and guidance in the areas of bibliographic description, automation, and electronic records. We thank her also for being both a tireless sounding board and a constant support throughout the project.

Others outside the committee also provided definitions and/or insights that helped make this glossary better than it would have been without them. Helen Samuels assisted us in preparing a definition for "documentation strategy." Alan F. Lewis sent us a number of terms and definitions in the fields of sound and moving images. Steve Hensen was extremely helpful with numerous terms, especially those relating to archival and bibliographic description. Toni Petersen and Cathy Whitehead of the J. Paul Getty Trust Art & Architecture Thesaurus Project were very helpful with terminology related to form, genre, and record type. Norman F. Boas assisted us in the world of manuscript abbreviations. Before this project we did not know an ALS from an AMuQS, and Dr. Boas helped dispel the darkness. In one case, associates of a committee member provided considerable assistance. Harold Naugler recruited a number of colleagues at the National Archives of Canada to review a draft of the volume. While we are unable to identify all by name, we do want to thank those we are able to identify: Sandra Wright, Philip Sylvain, Hugo Stibbe, and Denis Castonguay.

Last, but by no means least, were several others who were officially associated with the project. We wish in particular to thank Mary Jo Pugh, the Series Editor, for her many sound comments, her extensive editorial assistance, her patience, and her single-mindedness of purpose. Our drafts were presented to other manual authors, and we are indebted to two in particular who provided us with lengthy comments and assistance: James O'Toole and Mary Lynn Ritzenthaler. In addition there were two readers whose identity is unknown to us, but who provided many useful comments. We also acknowledge the solid practicality of Teresa Brinati at the SAA Office who provided valuable technical advice.

Lewis J. Bellardo
Lynn Lady Bellardo

Authors' Preface

In 1974 the Society of American Archivists (SAA) issued its "Basic Glossary" (cited in the bibliography on page 43 under Evans et al.). Since then the SAA glossary has served as a standard vocabulary for North American archivists, manuscript curators, and records managers. It remains an important tool, and the reader will find numerous similarities between this volume and the earlier work. There also have been many changes in practice and terminology during the intervening years, and we have endeavored to update the glossary to reflect these developments.

As with the earlier work, our goal is to provide archivists, manuscript curators, and records managers with a common vocabulary, and to acquaint entering professionals and outside audiences with the terminology of these three closely related professional groups. In addition, as noted by one of our readers, such a compilation of terminology serves to mark the current limits of professional concerns and responsibilities. When taken with earlier and future compilations, it may also serve to document the evolution of the three professional groups, their changing relationships, and their influence on one another over time.

The earlier SAA glossary was purposefully basic in its scope. We have attempted to be more inclusive in our selection of terms. We have not, however, attempted to produce a compendium of all terminology used in the various subspecialties represented here. There are good published glossaries and treatises that deal with specialized terminology in such areas as preservation, the USMARC AMC format, filing, diplomatics, and indexing. A number of these sources are identified in the bibliography. In general, we did not include terms if professional usage was clearly the same as the standard dictionary meaning. A significant exception is the inclusion of a number of document types. Since documents are fundamental to our work as professionals, we believe that the inclusion of such terms and definitions will prove useful to our readers. We did not include terms controlled by other professions unless the terms appeared to have special importance for archivists, manuscript curators, or records managers.

We have sought to represent fairly and adequately all three professional groups represented here. We also have attempted to reflect practice in both Canada and the United States, and to note clearly divergent practices between the two countries. Also included are a few European and Australian terms that represent significant concepts for which there are no equivalent North American terms.

As with both the earlier SAA glossary and the more recent glossary produced by the International Council on Archives, we have identified preferred terms and developed definitions reflecting the practices of leading archival institutions and professionals. The authors of the earlier SAA glossary stated that "because of the . . . conviction that professionalism demands precision, which in turn implies standardization, this glossary presents the preferred term and meaning in each case." We have opted wherever possible to follow this same precept in an effort to continue the process of refining terminology. At times, in the interest of clarity, we have drawn distinctions somewhat more sharply than others might. It is our hope in such cases to provoke additional discussion that might result in the further refinement of terminology.

The methodology underlying this glossary was an iterative process involving the authors, a variety of printed sources, and a number of our professional colleagues. Of utmost importance to us was a formal advisory committee, whose members included both generalists and specialists in a variety of fields. Their names are found at the front of this volume and in the Acknowledgments. Our first step was to consult printed sources and to draft a list of proposed terms and cross references. The committee members critiqued this draft and responded to an accompanying list of questions. The members added many useful terms, identified additional sources to examine, and suggested changes in our selections of preferred terms and cross references. They also indicated terms to be deleted, either because the terms were too specialized, or because their meaning was "self-evident" or the same as the standard dictionary meaning. In addition, a number of other colleagues submitted terms, and in some cases prepared draft definitions.

We next distilled the comments we received, revised the list of terms, and prepared a rough draft containing proposed definitions for the committee's consideration. This draft was also submitted to the manual authors and the editor of the Archival Fundamental series. In addition, we consulted other colleagues for perspectives on particular terms. The returns included much valuable assistance on style and substance. In some cases readers provided their own drafts of definitions, and in others they supplied new terms and definitions needed to fill gaps in our coverage. We integrated these comments and produced two more drafts that were each submitted for comment. The authors incorporated insights from these reviews into this final version.

During the course of this project we learned a great deal about the evolution of the three professional groups represented here. Like our predecessors on the earlier SAA glossary project, we kept the ideals of precision and standardization always in mind. However, we confess that there were numerous instances in which the ideal remained beyond our grasp. We spent countless hours trying to reconcile differences in usage among recognized professional leaders. At times we perceived a deterioration, rather than an improvement, in terminology since the earlier glossary was issued. Even the meanings of such fundamental terms as "archivist" and "archives" seemed in dispute!

From this period of pessimism, we emerged with an understanding that the work of archivists, records managers, and manuscript curators has been evolving, and continues to undergo development and change. Archivists are reaching out anew to records management, while manuscript curators and archivists are managing their materials in increasingly similar ways. Records management is merging with information management, and the possibilities and constraints posed by the computer pervade all disciplines. As a result, professional boundaries are blurring, the terminology of the three professions is rapidly changing and blending, and in many cases nomenclature is less clear than a generation ago. We have attempted to deal with this situation by providing for a number of terms both the narrower, traditional definition, as well as a broader, sometimes more diffuse definition that appears to be gaining in usage.

Given continuing changes in terminology, we recommend that the major national and international organizations representing archivists, manuscript curators, and records managers establish standing committees on terminology and mechanisms to ensure continuing liaison among those organizations. We also recommend that this glossary be revised frequently to reflect ongoing changes in professional nomenclature. Lastly, we urge educators to continue to emphasize instruction in terminology as an essential basis for professional development.

In closing, we reiterate that the professional groups represented here are far from fixing on a universally accepted body of nomenclature. That goal is probably not achievable. Nevertheless, it is our hope that this glossary is a step in the direction of standardization, that it accurately reflects the current universe of terminology, and that it will serve as a stimulus for further debate in those areas where greater clarification is needed.

Introduction

The body of the glossary consists of terms arranged alphabetically. Preferred terms appear entirely in upper case followed by definitions; non-preferred terms appear in upper and lower case with cross references to preferred terms. Terms found in upper case within a definition are defined elsewhere in the glossary. A number in parentheses follows such a term if the appropriate meaning is other than the first definition provided for the term. Thus, ARCHIVES appearing in the definition of another term directs the reader to the first meaning of "archives" in the glossary, while ARCHIVES (2) directs the reader to the second meaning. In the few cases where both the first and another meaning are intended, the numbers for all intended meanings are provided. Thus, RECORD (1,2) directs the reader to both the first and second meanings.

The order of definitions under a preferred term does not indicate degree of preference for the definitions: all definitions are acceptable. Occasionally, narrower meanings are followed by broader ones, and occasionally older meanings are followed by those that have emerged more recently. Nevertheless, all meanings provided under a term are valid, unless there is a specific statement to the contrary.

Cross references are of two types: "See" references refer the reader from a nonpreferred term to a preferred term. "See also" references are used with preferred terms to alert the reader to the existence of related terms. In a few cases, "See" references are used to bring together narrower terms under a broader term under which all are defined.

Following the glossary is an appendix that lists and defines abbreviations used by manuscript dealers and collectors, and that are encountered in the administration of historical and literary manuscripts. A few abbreviations convey meanings that diverge from the definitions found in this glossary, and the authors have noted such discrepancies. The volume concludes with a bibliography that directs readers to specialized glossaries and other sources that relate to the terminology of the three fields considered here.

Glossary authors sometimes employ "waffle" words or phrases to cover gaps in terminology, and the authors of this volume acknowledge their use of one. The expression "archival materials" is used to refer generically to materials housed in an archives or manuscript repository. The expression refers to both organic accumulations and to materials of mixed provenance purposefully gathered together by repositories. Since many repositories house both kinds of materials, and since many concepts apply to both as well, the authors felt some generic expression was necessary. "Manuscripts" is generic, but doesn't work because it cannot easily be stretched to include magnetic tapes and optical discs. "Archival materials" is a phrase increasingly being used, but it is not yet in so widespread use as to be enshrined as a "term."

Many sources have been consulted in compiling this glossary, and the definitions provided here often do not correspond identically to those in any of the sources. Published sources used to develop definitions have been cited in the bibliography. Definitions taken word-for-word from other sources include abbreviated citations in parentheses. The abbreviations used are:

AAT	Petersen, Toni, ed. *Art & Architecture Thesaurus.* New York: Oxford University Press for the J. Paul Getty Trust, 1990.
AHCDS	International Council on Archives, Ad Hoc Commission on Descriptive Standards. *Statement of Principles Regarding Archival Description,* draft. Ottawa: ICA, 1990.
ALA	Young, Heartsill, ed. *The ALA Glossary of Library and Information Science.* Chicago: American Library Association, 1983.
ARMA	Association of Records Managers and Administrators, Inc. *Glossary of Records Management Terms.* Prairie Village, Kansas: ARMA, 1985.

BLACKS   Black, Henry Campbell. *Black's Law Dictionary: Definitions of the Terms and Phrases of American and English Jurisprudence, Ancient and Modern,* 5th ed. St. Paul, Minnesota: West Publishing Co., 1979.

FRMGLOSS   National Archives and Records Administration, Office of Records Administration, Agency Services Division. *A Federal Records Management Glossary.* [Washington]: National Archives and Records Administration, 1989.

HARRODS   *Harrod's Librarians' Glossary of Terms Used in Librarianship, Documentation, and the Book Crafts and Reference Book,* 5th ed., revised and updated by Ray Prytherch; Leonard Montague Harrod, advisory editor. Brookfield, Vermont: Gower Publishing Company, 1984.

ICA   Evans, Frank B., Francois-J. Himly, and Peter Walne, comps.; and Peter Walne, ed. *Dictionary of Archival Terminology,* ICA Handbooks Series, volume 3. New York, London, Paris: K. G. Saur Munchen, 1984.

RAD   Bureau of Canadian Archivists, Planning Committee on Descriptive Standards. *Rules For Archival Description.* Ottawa: Bureau of Canadian Archivists, 1990.

SAA   Evans, Frank B., Donald F. Harrison, and Edwin A. Thompson, comps.; and William L. Rofes, ed. "A Basic Glossary for Archivists, Manuscript Curators, and Records Managers." *American Archivist* 37 (July 1974): 415–433.

UN   United Nations. *Management of Electronic Records: Issues and Guidelines.* New York: United Nations, 1990.

AACR 2 *See:* ANGLO-AMERICAN CATALOGUING RULES

ABSTRACT Brief summary of the essential points of a DOCUMENT. *See also:* BRIEF; EXTRACT; SCOPE AND CONTENT NOTE

ACCELERATED AGING TEST A laboratory test performed to determine within a relatively short time the ability of a material to withstand the deteriorating effects of aging.

ACCESS 1. Right, opportunity, or means of finding, using, or approaching DOCUMENTS and/or information.
2. In DATA PROCESSING, the process of retrieving DATA from memory.

ACCESS DATE The date at which DOCUMENTS become available for consultation by the general public, usually determined by the lapse of a specified number of years.

ACCESS POINT A name, term, phrase, or code that is used to search, identify, or locate a RECORD (1,2), FILE (1,2,3), or DOCUMENT (1,2).

ACCESS POLICY An official statement issued by an ARCHIVES (3) or MANUSCRIPT REPOSITORY specifying the conditions of ACCESS to its HOLDINGS. It is usually written and publicly available.

Access Restrictions *See:* RESTRICTED ACCESS

ACCESSIBILITY The availability of archival materials for consultation. ACCESSIBILITY can be determined by such factors as legal authorization, proximity of materials to RESEARCHERS, usable formats, and the existence of FINDING AIDS. *See also:* CLEARANCE; RESTRICTED ACCESS; SECURITY CLASSIFICATION

ACCESSION 1. The formal acceptance into CUSTODY of an ACQUISITION, and the recording of such act.
2. An ACQUISITION so recorded. *See also:* ACCRUAL

Accession Checklist *See:* CHECKLIST

ACCESSION LIST/REGISTER The DOCUMENT in which ACCESSIONS (2) are recorded, usually in chronological order by date of receipt, and giving the source and other identifying information for each ACCESSION (2).

ACCESSION NUMBER The unique number assigned serially to an ACCESSION (2).

ACCOUNT A DOCUMENT in which monies or goods received and paid or given out are recorded in order to permit periodic totaling. (AAT)

ACCOUNT BOOK A book in which financial accounts are kept. (AAT)

Accretion *See:* ACCRUAL

ACCRUAL An ACQUISITION additional to SERIES already held. An ACCRUAL is also called an accretion. *See also:* ACCESSION (2)

ACCUMULATION The natural process by which ARCHIVES are created in the conduct of affairs of any kind. The process is usually characterized as a "natural" or "organic" accumulation, in contrast to the purposeful gathering of "artificial" COLLECTIONS.

ACID MIGRATION The movement of acid from an acidic material to material of lesser or no acidity, either from direct contact or through exposure to acidic vapors in the surrounding environment.

ACID-FREE PAPER PAPER having a pH of 7.0 or greater. Unless treated with an alkaline substance capable of neutralizing acids, PAPER that is acid-free at the time of manufacture may become acidic through contact with acidic material or atmospheric pollutants. *See also:* ALKALINE RESERVE PAPER

Acidity *See:* pH

ACQUISITION An addition to the HOLDINGS of a RECORDS CENTER, ARCHIVES (2), or MANUSCRIPT REPOSITORY, whether received by TRANSFER under an established and legally based procedure, by DEPOSIT, purchase, GIFT, or BEQUEST. *See also:* ACCESSION (2)

ACQUISITION MICROFILM MICROFILM produced or acquired by an ARCHIVES (3) or MANUSCRIPT REPOSITORY to supplement and complement its own HOLDINGS. *See also:* DISPOSAL MICROFILMING; PRESERVATION MICROFILMING; SECURITY MICROFILMING

ACQUISITION POLICY An official statement issued by an ARCHIVES (3) or MANUSCRIPT REPOSITORY identifying the kinds of materials it accepts and the conditions or terms which affect their ACQUISITION. It serves as a basic DOCUMENT for the guidance of archival staff and organizations and persons interested in depositing their RECORDS or PAPERS.

ACT A DOCUMENT formally embodying a decision of a legislative body or a public authority; or forming part of a legal TRANSACTION and drawn up in due form. (ICA)

Active Records *See:* CURRENT RECORDS

ADDED ENTRY An ACCESS POINT other than a MAIN ENTRY in a DESCRIPTIVE RECORD. *See also:* ENTRY (2)

Addition *See:* ACCRUAL

ADMINISTRATIVE CONTROL The use of DOCUMEN-TATION to manage HOLDINGS as materials in the CUSTODY of a RECORDS CENTER, ARCHIVES (3), or MANUSCRIPT REPOSITORY without reference to the information they contain. *See also:* INTELLEC-TUAL CONTROL; PHYSICAL CONTROL; PROCESS CONTROL

ADMINISTRATIVE HISTORY That part of a FINDING AID that presents the history of the organiza-tion(s) that created or accumulated the material described therein, focusing on its/their structure and functional responsibilities over time. *See also:* BIOGRAPHICAL NOTE

ADMINISTRATIVE MICROFILMING The use of MI-CROFILM in the creation and/or use of CURRENT RECORDS. (ICA)

ADMINISTRATIVE RECORDS RECORDS that relate to the administration of finance, personnel, equipment, and other facilitative operations, as distinct from substantive or PROGRAM RECORDS. In Canada, ADMINISTRATIVE RECORDS are re-ferred to as housekeeping records and include five categories: administrative, building and properties, equipment and supplies, finance, and personnel.

ADMINISTRATIVE REGULATION In government, a regulation issued by an AGENCY, having the force of law, to interpret or implement the provisions of a STATUTE.

ADMINISTRATIVE VALUE The usefulness of REC-ORDS/ARCHIVES for the conduct of current and/or future administrative business. Administrative value is also called operational value. *See also:* FISCAL VALUE; LEGAL VALUE

Administratively Controlled Information/Records *See:* RESTRICTED INFORMATION/RECORDS

AERIAL PHOTOGRAPH A PHOTOGRAPH taken from a predetermined altitude and in accordance with a plan and scale.

AGENCY An organizational entity whose name and legal existence are established by an ACT, which defines its position in an administrative hierar-chy. Such a body possesses powers defined by law or regulations and a head with decision-making authority at his/her hierarchical level. Usually, each agency has its own recordkeeping system. *See also:* CORPORATE BODY

Agency History *See:* ADMINISTRATIVE HISTORY

Agency Records Center *See:* RECORDS CENTER

AGREEMENT A writing made to evidence the terms and conditions, or the fact, of an accord or ar-rangement. (AAT)

AISLE Passageway between two ROWS of shelving providing ACCESS to the shelves.

ALBUM A book of blank leaves in which literary EXTRACTS, quotations, poems, DRAWINGS, PHOTO-GRAPHS, or other ITEMS are written, inserted, or affixed.

ALIENATION 1. In a strict legal sense, the transfer of ownership of property.
2. In general archival usage, the TRANSFER or loss of CUSTODY of RECORDS/ARCHIVES by their custodian or owner to someone not legally enti-tled to them. *See also:* ESTRAY; REMOVED AR-CHIVES; REPLEVIN

ALKALINE RESERVE PAPER PAPER having an alka-line reserve or buffer. The alkaline BUFFERING AGENT counteracts acid which might develop later from contact with acidic materials or atmo-spheric pollution. *See also:* ACID-FREE PAPER

Alphabetical Arrangement *See:* ARRANGEMENT

AMC Format *See:* USMARC FORMAT FOR ARCHIVAL AND MANUSCRIPTS CONTROL (USMARC AMC)

Analog Videodisc *See:* VIDEODISC

Analytical Index *See:* CLASSIFIED INDEX

ANALYTICAL INVENTORY A very detailed INVEN-TORY in which DOCUMENTS are described at the FILE and, often, ITEM level.

ANGLO-AMERICAN CATALOGUING RULES (AACR) Standards and rules adopted by the li-brary profession for the description of materials. In 1988, the American Library Association is-sued *AACR 2*, Revised. *See also: ARCHIVES, PER-SONAL PAPERS, AND MANUSCRIPTS*, 2ND EDITION (*APPM*)

APERTURE CARD A card, usually punched and of a size and shape suitable for use in DATA PRO-CESSING systems, with one or more rectangular holes specifically designed to hold a FRAME or FRAMES of MICROFILM. *See also:* PUNCHED CARD/TAPE

APPM *See: ARCHIVES, PERSONAL PAPERS, AND MANU-SCRIPTS*, 2ND EDITION (*APPM*)

APPRAISAL The process of determining the value and thus the DISPOSITION of RECORDS based upon their current administrative, legal, and fiscal use; their EVIDENTIAL and INFORMATIONAL VALUE; their ARRANGEMENT and condition; THEIR INTRINSIC VALUE; and their relationship to other RECORDS.

Appraisal (Monetary) *See:* VALUATION

Aqueous Deacidification *See:* DEACIDIFICATION

ARCHIVAL ADMINISTRATION The management or direction of the program of an ARCHIVES (3) or MANUSCRIPT REPOSITORY, including the following archival functions: APPRAISAL and DISPOSITION, ACQUISITION, ARRANGEMENT, DESCRIPTION, PRESERVATION, REFERENCE SERVICE, OUTREACH, and other user services.

Archival Agency *See:* ARCHIVES (3)

Archival and Manuscripts Control Format (AMC) *See:* USMARC FORMAT FOR ARCHIVAL AND MANUSCRIPTS CONTROL (USMARC AMC)

Archival Arrangement *See:* ARRANGEMENT

Archival Description *See:* DESCRIPTION (1,2)

Archival Holdings *See:* HOLDINGS

ARCHIVAL INTEGRITY The principle that a FONDS or RECORD GROUP must be preserved without division, mutilation, ALIENATION (2), unauthorized DESTRUCTION or any addition, except by ACCRUAL or REPLEVIN, in order to ensure its full EVIDENTIAL and INFORMATIONAL VALUE. The concept of ARCHIVAL INTEGRITY derives from the principles of PROVENANCE and RESPECT FOR ORIGINAL ORDER. *See also:* FILE INTEGRITY; PROVENANCE (PRINCIPLE OF)

Archival Institution *See:* ARCHIVES (3)

ARCHIVAL JURISDICTION The sphere of responsibility of an ARCHIVES (3), as defined by law, regulations, or policies.

Archival Management *See:* ARCHIVAL ADMINISTRATION

ARCHIVAL NATURE In Canada, the characteristics which are given to archival DOCUMENTS by the circumstances of their creation and are therefore natural to them. They are: naturalness (archival DOCUMENTS are natural ACCUMULATIONS), organicity or inter-relationship (archival DOCUMENTS are functionally related to each other within and outside each given FONDS), impartiality (DOCUMENTS are a means for carrying out activities and, therefore, should accurately reflect the activities they document), authenticity (archival DOCUMENTS are authentic with respect to their CREATOR), and uniqueness (each DOCUMENT is related to the others within and outside the FONDS of which it is a part, and to the CREATOR of the FONDS by a special relationship, which makes it unique).

ARCHIVAL QUALITY 1. The material properties inherent in any MEDIUM permitting its preservation under controlled conditions.
2. In Canada, the archival characteristics, such as interrelationship, which documentary material that is non-archival as to the circumstances of creation acquires when it becomes part of a living archival FONDS. For example, a book becoming part of a court's FILES related to a trial for COPYRIGHT has archival quality.

Archival Repository *See:* ARCHIVES (2)

ARCHIVAL STUDIES The whole of the knowledge that belongs to and identifies the professional ARCHIVIST, including theory, practice, and scholarship, as established in formal curricula of study.

ARCHIVAL SUCCESSION The succession of legal jurisdiction over government ARCHIVES as the result of changes in territorial sovereignty.

ARCHIVAL TEACHING UNIT A selection of FACSIMILES of DOCUMENTS, copies of PHOTOGRAPHS and MAPS, and explanatory materials relating to some historical period, event, movement, or person to be used in the classroom by teachers and students.

ARCHIVAL VALUE Those values—administrative, fiscal, legal, intrinsic, evidential, and/or informational—which justify the PRESERVATION of RECORDS/ARCHIVES.

ARCHIVES 1. The DOCUMENTS created or received and accumulated by a person or organization in the course of the conduct of affairs, and preserved because of their continuing value. Historically, the term referred more narrowly to the NONCURRENT RECORDS of an organization or institution preserved because of their continuing value.
2. The building or part of a building where archival materials are located; also referred to as an archival repository.
3. The AGENCY or program responsible for selecting, acquiring, preserving, and making available archival materials; also referred to as an archival agency, archival institution, or archival program.

ARCHIVES BOX/CONTAINER A storage container, variable in terms of composition, construction, and dimensions, intended to protect and facilitate the handling of archival materials. Archives boxes are also called manuscript boxes. *See also:* RECORDS CENTER CARTON/CONTAINER

ARCHIVES, PERSONAL PAPERS, AND MANUSCRIPTS, 2ND EDITION (APPM) A manual for archival cataloging, particularly at the COLLECTION (1,2), RECORD GROUP, or FONDS level, endorsed by the Society of American Archivists. The manual is a modification of the standards/guidelines in *AACR 2. See also: ANGLO-AMERICAN CATALOGING RULES (AACR)*

ARCHIVIST A person professionally educated, trained, experienced, and engaged in the administration of archival materials, including the following activities: APPRAISAL and DISPOSITION, ACQUISITION, PRESERVATION, ARRANGEMENT and DESCRIPTION, REFERENCE SERVICE, and OUTREACH. In the United States, the term is also frequently used to refer to a MANUSCRIPT CURATOR. *See also:* RECORDS MANAGER

ARRANGEMENT The intellectual and physical processes and results of organizing DOCUMENTS in accordance with accepted archival principles, particularly PROVENANCE, at as many as necessary of the following levels: REPOSITORY, COLLECTION, RECORD GROUP or FONDS, SUBGROUP(S), SERIES, SUBSERIES, file unit, and ITEM. The processes usually include packing, LABELING, and shelving and are primarily intended to achieve PHYSICAL CONTROL over archival HOLDINGS. *See also:* LEVELS OF ARRANGEMENT; PROCESSING

ARTICLES OF INCORPORATION A written AGREEMENT embodying the purposes and conditions of the association of a number of persons for the pursuit of a joint enterprise; especially those duly executed and filed with a state's administrative authorities so as to have the force of a CHARTER under general incorporation law.

Artifactual Value *See:* INTRINSIC VALUE

Artificial Collection *See:* COLLECTION

AUDIOTAPE SOUND RECORDINGS on MAGNETIC TAPE. (ICA)

AUDIO-VISUAL RECORDS/ARCHIVES RECORDS/ ARCHIVES in pictorial and/or aural form, regardless of FORMAT. *See also:* FILM RECORDS/ARCHIVES; ICONOGRAPHIC RECORDS/ARCHIVES; PHOTOGRAPHIC RECORDS/ARCHIVES

AUTHENTICATION The act of verifying that a DOCUMENT or a REPRODUCTION of a DOCUMENT is what it purports to be. *See also:* CERTIFICATION

AUTHORITY CONTROL The process of verifying and authorizing the choice of unique ACCESS POINTS, such as names, subjects, and FORMS (3), and ensuring that the ACCESS POINTS are consistently applied and maintained in an information retrieval system. *See also:* AUTHORITY FILE; AUTHORITY RECORD; CONTROLLED VOCABULARY

Authority Entry *See:* AUTHORITY RECORD

AUTHORITY FILE A group of AUTHORITY RECORDS searchable by all established HEADINGS (2) and CROSS-REFERENCES. *See also:* CONTROLLED VOCABULARY; THESAURUS

Authority List *See:* AUTHORITY FILE

AUTHORITY RECORD An ENTRY (2) that contains information about an ACCESS POINT. An authority record establishes the form of the HEADING (2), determines CROSS-REFERENCES and the relationships of the HEADING (2) to other HEADINGS (2) in the AUTHORITY FILE, and documents the decisions. *See also:* AUTHORITY CONTROL

AUTOGRAPH 1. A personal SIGNATURE.
2. A MANUSCRIPT, signed or unsigned, in the hand of the author. (ICA)
3. A TYPESCRIPT signed by the author. *See also:* HOLOGRAPH

Automated Records *See:* MACHINE-READABLE RECORDS/ARCHIVES

AUTOMATED TECHNIQUES The use of automation to assist in the performance of archival functions.

Automatic Data Processing (ADP) *See:* DATA PROCESSING

AUTOMATIC INDEXING A method of indexing by which a computer is used to select from a DOCUMENT the terms to be used as the HEADINGS (2) of index ENTRIES. *See also:* COMPUTER-BASED INDEXING

Automatic Posting *See:* POSTING UP

BACK-TO-BACK ROWS/SHELVING Two ROWS of shelving with their backs immediately adjacent to each other along their long axes.

Backup Copy *See:* SECURITY COPY

BALANCE SHEET A statement of the financial condition, as of a corporation, at a given date showing the equality of total assets to total liabilities plus net worth, or of total liabilities to total assets plus deficit. (AAT)

BAR CODE A coding system consisting of vertical lines or bars which, when read by an optical SCANNER, can be converted to machine-readable language.

BARRIER SHEET A sheet, such as polyester or alkaline buffered PAPER, placed between materials to retard ACID MIGRATION.

BATCH PROCESSING In DATA PROCESSING, a technique by which items to be processed must be coded and collected into groups prior to processing. *See also:* OFF-LINE PROCESSING; ON-LINE PROCESSING

BAY A unit of shelving, single or double sided, consisting of horizontal SHELVES between standards,

UPRIGHTS, or upright frames. A bay is also called a compartment. *See also:* BACK-TO-BACK ROWS/SHELVING

BEQUEST The transfer of CUSTODY and title to DOCUMENTS by last WILL and testament. (ICA)

BIBLIOGRAPHIC DESCRIPTION A written representation that characterizes a UNIT OF DESCRIPTION by means of DATA ELEMENTS (such as CREATOR, dates, and CONTENT) that are organized according to the provisions of a standard and treated as a logical unit. A bibliographic description acts as a surrogate for the unit it describes.

BINDING 1. The permanent fastening together, usually between covers, of manuscript or printed SHEETS to keep them in a fixed order and to assist in protecting them. (ICA)
2. The cover in 1 above. (ICA)

BIOGRAPHICAL NOTE That part of a FINDING AID which records the highlights of the life and activities of a person or family that generated the DOCUMENTS described therein. *See also:* ADMINISTRATIVE HISTORY

BLUEPRINT A PRINT made on PAPER or cloth, coated with light-sensitive iron salts, producing an IMAGE in white on a blue background. The process has most frequently been used for copying such DOCUMENTS as MAPS, mechanical drawings, and architects' plans.

BOND 1. A written obligation to indemnify for a loss suffered or for the failure to perform in some specified manner.
2. A CERTIFICATE of debt.

Book Catalog *See:* CATALOG

BOOLEAN LOGIC A method of inquiry used in INFORMATION RETRIEVAL SYSTEMS that includes the logical operators, "and," "or," "not," "except," "if," and "then," which may be combined in a variety of ways.

Box *See:* ARCHIVES BOX/CONTAINER; RECORDS CENTER CARTON/CONTAINER

Box List *See:* CONTAINER LIST

BRIEF 1. A summary, ABSTRACT, or abridgment of a DOCUMENT. (ICA)
2. A summary of the facts of a case with special reference to the points of law involved to assist in presenting the case before a court of law. (ICA)
3. An open LETTER issued by the papal chancery, sealed with a wax SEAL (2). (ICA)
4. A LETTER issued by a lawful authority to an individual or institution commanding the performance of a specified action. Such a DOCUMENT is also called a writ. (ICA)

BRITTLENESS A condition in which PAPER or another MEDIUM breaks rather than bends when flexed. Brittleness usually results from the effects of acidity in the MEDIUM, aggravated by heat, light, and/or aging. The concept is usually used in the adjective form, as in brittle or embrittled paper.

BROADER TERM In a THESAURUS, a term that denotes a concept wider in scope than one with a more specific meaning. For example, "Science" is broader than "Physics." *See also:* NARROWER TERM; RELATED TERM

Broadsheet *See:* BROADSIDE

BROADSIDE A publication consisting of a single sheet (or less frequently, of a few conjoining sheets) bearing information printed as a single PAGE, on one side only of the sheet; usually intended to be posted, publicly distributed, or sold (e.g., proclamations, handbills, newssheet, sheet calendars).

BROWNPRINT A PRINT made on a light-sensitized surface that produces a white IMAGE on a brown background. (AAT)

BUFFERING AGENT An alkaline substance intended to counteract existing acid or the formation of acid in PAPER. *See also:* ALKALINE RESERVE PAPER; PERMANENT/DURABLE PAPER; pH

BULK DATES Dates of those DOCUMENTS that constitute the largest part of a COLLECTION, RECORD GROUP, SUBGROUP, or SERIES. Bulk dates are used to inform RESEARCHERS of the chronological or period strength of archival materials, particularly when INCLUSIVE DATES are misleading.

Bulk Reduction Microfilming *See:* DISPOSAL MICROFILMING

BUNDLE A storage unit consisting of a number of individual DOCUMENTS, normally tied together by string, tape, or the like.

CADASTRAL MAP A MAP showing boundaries of subdivisions of land for purposes of describing and recording ownership as a basis for taxation.

CADASTRE An official statement of the quantity and value of real property in any district, made for the purpose of apportioning the taxes payable on such property.

CALENDAR A chronological list of individual DOCU-MENTS, either selective or comprehensive, usually with a description providing such information as writer, recipient, date, place, summary of CONTENT, type of DOCUMENT, and PAGE or LEAF count.

Captured Archives *See:* REMOVED ARCHIVES

CAR *See:* COMPUTER-ASSISTED RETRIEVAL (CAR)

CARBON COPY A COPY of a DOCUMENT created simultaneously with the original MANUSCRIPT or TYPESCRIPT by the use of an intermediate sheet of carbon paper or of self-carboned paper. (ICA)

Card Catalog *See:* CATALOG

Card Index *See:* INDEX

CARTOGRAPHIC RECORDS/ARCHIVES RECORDS/ARCHIVES containing information depicting in graphic or photogrammetric form, a portion of the linear surface of the earth or of a heavenly body, such as MAPS, CHARTS, PLANS, and related materials (globes, topographic and hydrographic CHARTS, cartograms, relief models, and AERIAL PHOTOGRAPHS).

CARTRIDGE A closed container of FILM or of MAGNETIC TAPE, designed for loading and unloading in a READER, projector, recorder, or computer tape drive, without prior threading or rewinding. A double-cored cartridge is called a CASSETTE. (ICA) *See also:* OPEN REEL FILM/TAPE

CARTULARY An assemblage, usually in volume form, of CHARTERS, title DEEDS, and other DOCUMENTS of significance belonging to a person, family, or organization.

CASE FILE A FILE (1,2) relating to a specific action, event, person, place, project, or other subject. A case file is sometimes referred to as a project file or dossier; in Canadian usage, as a transactional file.

CASH BOOK A book of original ENTRY in which a record is kept of all cash receipts, disbursements, or both. (AAT)

CASSETTE A device containing FILM or MAGNETIC TAPE, a supply spool, and a take-up spool, all within a protective housing. *See also:* CARTRIDGE; OPEN REEL FILM/TAPE

CATALOG A listing of materials with descriptive details, usually arranged systematically. Catalogs are produced in a variety of formats, including book, card, MICROFORM, or electronic. In Canada, catalogue.

CD-ROM *See:* COMPACT DISC

CELLULOSE NITRATE FILM A flexible support or base used for photographic NEGATIVES and motion picture film from c. 1890 to c. 1950. It is very unstable and highly flammable, representing a major fire hazard. Cellulose nitrate film is commonly recopied onto another MEDIUM, such as SAFETY FILM.

CENTRAL FILES The RECORDS or FILES of one or more organizational units physically and/or functionally centralized.

Central Records *See:* CENTRAL FILES

Central Registry *See:* REGISTRY

CERTIFICATE A DOCUMENT giving authoritative recognition of a fact, qualification, or promise. (AAT)

CERTIFICATION The formal assertion, in writing, of some fact. *See also:* AUTHENTICATION; CERTIFIED COPY

CERTIFIED COPY A COPY of a DOCUMENT signed and certified as a true copy by the official custodian of the ORIGINAL DOCUMENT. *See also:* AUTHENTICATION; CERTIFICATION

Chain of Custody *See:* CUSTODIAL HISTORY

CHARGE-OUT 1. The act of recording the removal of DOCUMENTS from storage.
2. The DOCUMENT used to record the above action.

Charge-Out Guide *See:* OUT-GUIDE

CHART 1. A writing exhibiting tabulated or methodically arranged information.
2. A cartographic DOCUMENT, usually referring to water, air, or astronomical objects.

CHARTER A DOCUMENT, usually sealed, granting specific rights, setting forth aims and principles of a newly established entity, and often embodying formal agreements and authorizing special privileges or exemptions. (AAT)

CHECKLIST A list of DOCUMENTS prepared for purposes of identification and control. *See also:* TRANSMITTAL LIST

Chron/Chrono File *See:* CHRONOLOGICAL FILE

Chronological Arrangement *See:* ARRANGEMENT

CHRONOLOGICAL FILE A FILE (2) containing DOCUMENTS or copies of DOCUMENTS arranged in chronological order. Such a FILE (2) is also referred to as chron file, chrono file, day file, and in Canadian usage, a continuity file. If the FILE (2) is circulated for reference, it is also referred to as a reading file. If arranged from latest to earliest date, it is referred to as a reverse chronological file.

CHRONOLOGY 1. The science of measuring time in fixed periods and of identifying and comparing dates expressed in various styles or calendars. (ICA)
2. The selection and arrangement of dates and events. (ICA)

3. A DOCUMENT listing dates and events in chronological order.

CIM *See:* COMPUTER INPUT MICROFILM/MICROFORM (CIM)

Cinefilm *See:* MOTION PICTURE

CIPHER 1. A system of writing based on a key, or set of predetermined rules or symbols, used for secret communication. (ICA)
2. A message in such writing. (ICA)
3. The key to such a system of writing. Cipher is also referred to as code. (ICA)

Circulation Record *See:* CHARGE-OUT

CLASS 1. In CLASSIFICATION, a group of DOCUMENTS having common characteristics.
2. The functional category of a CLASSIFICATION PLAN/SCHEME.

CLASSIFICATION 1. Any method of recognizing relationships between DOCUMENTS.
2. The systematic identification and arrangement of DOCUMENTS in categories according to logically structured conventions, methods, and procedural rules represented in a CLASSIFICATION PLAN/SCHEME. *See also:* ARRANGEMENT; FILING SYSTEM; SECURITY CLASSIFICATION

CLASSIFICATION PLAN/SCHEME A diagram or table in which the DOCUMENTS of an organization are categorized according to a coding system expressed in symbols (i.e., alphabetical, numerical, alpha-numerical, or decimal). *See also:* FILING PLAN

CLASSIFIED INDEX An INDEX characterized by hierarchical structure, in which topics are grouped under broad subjects of which they form a part. A classified index is also called an analytical index.

Classified Information/Records *See:* SECURITY CLASSIFICATION

Cleaning: *See:* SURFACE CLEANING

CLEARANCE An administrative determination that an individual may have ACCESS to RESTRICTED INFORMATION/RECORDS of a specified category. (ICA) *See also:* RESTRICTED ACCESS

Closed Access *See:* RESTRICTED ACCESS

CLOSED FILE 1. A file unit or SERIES containing DOCUMENTS on which action has been completed and to which additional DOCUMENTS are not likely to be added. *See also:* OPEN FILE
2. A file unit or SERIES to which ACCESS is restricted or denied. *See also:* OPEN FILE (2); RESTRICTED INFORMATION/RECORDS; SECURITY CLASSIFICATION

CLOSED INDEX An INDEX to which no further entries may be added.

CLOSED RECORD GROUP A RECORD GROUP to which further RECORDS are not likely to be added because of the abolition of the creating body, major administrative reorganization, or basic change in the FILING PLAN or FILING SYSTEM.

Code *See:* CIPHER

COLLECTION 1. An artificial accumulation of DOCUMENTS brought together on the basis of some common characteristic (e.g., means of acquisition, CREATOR, subject, language, MEDIUM, FORM (2), name of collector) without regard to the PROVENANCE of the DOCUMENTS.
2. A grouping of RECORDS/ARCHIVES created by private individuals and organizations. *See also:* FAMILY (AND ESTATE) ARCHIVES; MANUSCRIPT GROUP; PAPERS; PERSONAL PAPERS; PRIVATE RECORDS/ARCHIVES
3. The total HOLDINGS of a MANUSCRIPT REPOSITORY.

Collection Development Policy *See:* ACQUISITION POLICY

Collection Policy *See:* ACQUISITION POLICY

COLLECTIVE RECORD GROUP A type of RECORD GROUP which, for convenience, brings together the RECORDS of a number of relatively small and/or short-lived AGENCIES that have an administrative or functional relationship, the RECORDS of each such AGENCY constituting a separate SUBGROUP. (ICA) *See also:* GENERAL RECORD GROUP

COM *See:* COMPUTER OUTPUT MICROFILM/MICROFORM (COM)

Common Records Schedule *See:* GENERAL RECORDS SCHEDULE

COMMONPLACE BOOK A book in which literary passages, cogent quotations, poems, comments, recipes, prescriptions, etc., are written.

COMPACT DISC A high-density digital disc data storage MEDIUM commonly used for publishing A compact disc that permits read-only ACCESS (2) is commonly referred to as CD-ROM (Compact Disc-Read Only Memory). Information is read by means of a laser. *See also:* OPTICAL DISC; VIDEODISC

COMPACT SHELVING A system of mobile shelving intended to save space and/or guarantee SECURITY comprising movable ROWS, operated manually, mechanically, electrically, or in combination, either horizontally on rails or rotating through a quarter-circle on a pivot.

Compact Storage *See:* COMPACT SHELVING

Compartment *See:* BAY

COMPETENCE The sphere of responsibility entrusted to a given officer or person. For example, the competence of an ARCHIVIST within an AR-CHIVES (3) may be restricted to a single FUNCTION, such as APPRAISAL. Conversely, it may include all archival FUNCTIONS for one or more FONDS or RECORD GROUPS. *See also:* FUNCTION; MANDATE

COMPLEX ENTRY An index entry that is inverted, has a qualifier, or is a phrase. (ARMA) *See also:* DIRECT ENTRY; INVERTED ENTRY

Comprehensive Records Plan *See:* RECORDS SCHEDULE

COMPUTER ASSISTED RETRIEVAL (CAR) The use of a computer to index and retrieve material not contained within that computer's data bank. This term is commonly applied to RETRIEVAL from MICROFILM.

COMPUTER-BASED INDEXING Indexing primarily or to a significant degree carried out by use of a computer. *See also:* AUTOMATIC INDEXING

COMPUTER INPUT MICROFILM/MICROFORM (CIM) The concept that computer input can be taken directly from MICROFILM/MICROFORM, by scanning and character recognition. The term also refers to the system of software and hardware that makes this method of transferring data to disk possible. *See also:* COMPUTER OUTPUT MICROFILM/MICROFORM (COM)

COMPUTER OUTPUT MICROFILM/MICROFORM (COM) Computer output produced directly onto MICROFILM/MICROFORM, without paper printout as an intermediary. The term may also be used to designate the equipment producing the MICRO-FORM or the process as a whole. *See also:* COM-PUTER INPUT MICROFILM/MICROFORM (CIM)

CONCEPT INDEXING The process of assigning index terms based on peripheral or background information contained in a DOCUMENT.

CONCORDANCE In archival usage, a FINDING AID in list form establishing the relationship between the past and present reference numbers of archival material that has been rearranged, relocated, or, simply, renumbered. A concordance is also called a conversion list.

CONFIDENTIALITY The quality of secrecy attaching to certain information and/or DOCUMENTS, that thereby require protection, usually taking the form of RESTRICTED ACCESS. *See also:* PRIVACY

CONSERVATION The component of PRESERVATION that deals with the physical or chemical treatment of DOCUMENTS. *See also:* REVERSIBILITY (PRINCIPLE OF)

CONSERVATION LABORATORY A workshop or laboratory in which DOCUMENTS are treated to physically support and/or chemically stabilize them.

CONSERVATOR A professional trained in the arts and sciences relating to the theoretical and practical aspects of preserving materials.

CONTACT COPY A COPY produced by holding a sheet of sensitized material in direct contact with the ORIGINAL DOCUMENT or photographic NEGATIVE during EXPOSURE to light.

CONTAINER LIST A listing of materials by container, meant to facilitate RETRIEVAL. A container list normally includes the title of the SE-RIES or FILE (2), the portion of the FILE (2) contained in each container, and the INCLUSIVE DATES of the materials contained therein. A container list may also include shelf locations for each container. *See also:* FOLDER LIST

CONTENT The information that a DOCUMENT is meant to convey, as opposed to FORM (2).

Content Note *See:* SCOPE AND CONTENT NOTE

CONTEXT 1. The organizational, functional, and operational circumstances in which DOCUMENTS are created and/or received and used.
2. The parts of a title or text that precede or follow the KEYWORD, usually influencing its meaning. *See also:* KEYWORD AND CONTEXT (KWAC); KEYWORD IN CONTEXT (KWIC); KEYWORD OUT OF CONTEXT (KWOC)

CONTINGENT RECORDS In DISPOSITION, RECORDS scheduled for final DISPOSITION after the occurrence of a particular event at an unspecified future time, such as the decommissioning of a naval vessel.

Continuing Value *See:* ARCHIVAL VALUE

Continuity File *See:* CHRONOLOGICAL FILE

CONTRACT A DOCUMENT, enforceable by law, embodying an agreement between two or more competent parties to do or not to do something, and specifying the terms and conditions of the agreement. (AAT)

CONTRAST An expression in photography of the relationship between the high and low brightness of a subject, or between the high and low DENSITY of a photographic IMAGE. (ICA)

CONTROLLED VOCABULARY A regularized or standardized list of terms used to increase uniformity in indexing or information retrieval. *See also:* AUTHORITY CONTROL; AUTHORITY FILE; THE-SAURUS

CONTROLLING AGENCY The AGENCY or other COR-PORATE BODY that exercises control over a group of RECORDS with respect to withdrawal and use for its FUNCTIONS, retention or DISPOSITION, and public ACCESS. A controlling agency may be the OFFICE OF ORIGIN, TRANSFERRING AGENCY, or its successor. *See also:* FUNCTIONAL SOVEREIGNTY (PRINCIPLE OF)

CONVENIENCE FILE Extra copies of DOCUMENTS maintained for ease of ACCESS and reference. A convenience file is sometimes known as a personal file or crutch file.

Conversion List *See:* CONCORDANCE

COORDINATE INDEXING SYSTEM An indexing system or scheme whereby the relationships of terms are shown by coupling individual words. *See also:* POST-COORDINATE INDEXING SYSTEM; PRE-COORDINATE INDEXING SYSTEM

COPY A duplication of a DOCUMENT prepared simultaneously or separately, usually identified by function or by method of creation. *See also:* CARBON COPY; CONTACT COPY; FACSIMILE; FAIR COPY; RECORD COPY

Copy, Carbon *See:* CARBON COPY

Copy, Certified *See:* CERTIFIED COPY

COPYRIGHT The right vested by law in the author of a DOCUMENT and his/her heirs or assignees to publish or reproduce the DOCUMENT or to authorize publication or REPRODUCTION thereof.

CORPORATE BODY An organization or group of persons that is identified by a particular name and that acts, or may act, as an entity. Examples are associations, business firms, churches, conferences, governments, government agencies, institutions, nonprofit organizations, and religious bodies.

CORRESPONDENCE Any form of addressed and written communication sent and received, including LETTERS, postcards, memoranda, NOTES, telegrams, or cables. (ICA)

CORRESPONDENCE MANAGEMENT The application of RECORDS MANAGEMENT principles and techniques to CORRESPONDENCE. In Canadian usage, correspondence management is known as treatment of correspondence. (ICA)

COUNTERSEAL A SEAL (2), usually smaller than and distinguished in design from the principal SEAL (2), impressed on the reverse of an impression of the principal SEAL (2) to give added validity and AUTHENTICATION to the DOCUMENT so validated.

COVER An envelope or outer wrapping that has passed through the mail and bears postal markings, such as STAMPS (2) or postmarks.

Creating Agency/Office *See:* OFFICE OF ORIGIN

CREATOR The person or organization that creates or receives and accumulates DOCUMENTS. *See*

also: CONTROLLING AGENCY; DONOR; OFFICE OF ORIGIN; TRANSFERRING AGENCY

CROSS-REFERENCE An ENTRY (2) directing attention to one or more HEADINGS (2).

Crutch File *See:* CONVENIENCE FILE

CUBIC FEET A measurement of VOLUME (2) for RECORDS, ARCHIVES, and MANUSCRIPTS. *See also:* LINEAR FEET

Culling *See:* WEEDING

CUMULATIVE INDEX An INDEX comprised of ENTRIES merged from previous indexes.

Curator *See:* MANUSCRIPT CURATOR

CURRENT RECORDS RECORDS regularly used for the conduct of the current business of their CREATOR and that, therefore, continue to be maintained in office space. In Canada, current records are known as active records. *See also:* NONCURRENT RECORDS; SEMICURRENT RECORDS

CUSTODIAL HISTORY The succession of offices or persons who had CUSTODY of a body of archival materials from its creation to its acquisition by an ARCHIVES (3) or MANUSCRIPT REPOSITORY. *See also:* PROVENANCE

CUSTODY The responsibility for the care of DOCUMENTS based on their physical possession. CUSTODY does not always include legal ownership, or the right to control ACCESS to RECORDS.

Cut-off *See:* FILE BREAK

DATA ARCHIVES An organization, or administrative unit thereof, responsible for the acquisition, preservation, and communication of data in electronic form, regardless of PROVENANCE. *See also:* ELECTRONIC RECORDS

DATA BASE Data organized and stored so that it can be manipulated or extracted to meet various applications but managed independently of them.

DATA DICTIONARY A structured assembly of information about the definition, structure, and use of data. It does not, however, contain the actual data itself. Specifically, the data dictionary contains the name of each DATA ELEMENT, its definition (size and type), where and how it is used, and its relationship to other data. *See also:* METADATA

DATA ELEMENT The smallest unit of data for which attributes are specified, generally corresponding to a FIELD in a data-processing RECORD (2) or a numbered box on a printed FORM. For example, name, address, series title, and record group number are all data elements.

DATA PROCESSING The systematic performance of an operation or sequence of operations upon data by one or more computer-processing units to achieve a desired end result. Data processing is used synonymously with information processing.

Data Record *See:* RECORD (2)

Data Set *See:* FILE (3)

Date Span *See:* INCLUSIVE DATES

Date Range *See:* INCLUSIVE DATES

DAY BOOK A VOLUME used in bookkeeping containing daily records of receipts and expenditures in order of their occurrence.

Day File *See:* CHRONOLOGICAL FILE

DEACCESSIONING The process by which an ARCHIVES (3) or MANUSCRIPT REPOSITORY formally removes material from its CUSTODY. An archival institution may deaccession material because the material has been reappraised and found to be unsuitable for its HOLDINGS, the legal owner has requested permanent return of the materials, or the institution has agreed to transfer the materials to another REPOSITORY. *See also:* REAPPRAISAL

DEACIDIFICATION The process by which the acid in PAPER is neutralized so that the pH value is at least 7.0, thereby assisting in PRESERVATION. Normally, the process deposits an alkaline buffer or reserve to inhibit the return of an acidic state. Common forms of deacidification include: (a) aqueous deacidification, which uses water as the solvent carrier of the alkaline agent; (b) non-aqueous deacidification, which uses organic solvents as the solvent carrier; (c) vapor phase deacidification, which involves the INTERLEAVING of DOCUMENTS and the PAGES of VOLUMES with treated sheets that emit an alkaline vapor (now rarely used because it reportedly produces toxic vapors and does not leave an alkaline reserve); (d) mass deacidification, which refers to one of various techniques designed to treat large numbers of DOCUMENTS at one time with either gaseous or liquid agents.

DECLASSIFICATION The removal of all SECURITY CLASSIFICATION restrictions on information or RECORDS. (ICA) *See also:* DOWNGRADE

DEED A DOCUMENT, usually under SEAL, by which one party conveys property, especially real estate, to another. A deed differs from a CONTRACT in that a deed is a mere transfer of title and is the act of but one party, made pursuant to a previous CONTRACT.

DEED OF GIFT A signed, written INSTRUMENT containing a voluntary transfer of title to real or personal property without a monetary consideration. Deeds of gift to ARCHIVES (3) or MANUSCRIPT REPOSITORIES frequently take the form of a CONTRACT establishing conditions governing the transfer of title to DOCUMENTS and specifying any restrictions on ACCESS or use. A deed of gift is also known as an instrument of gift.

DEHUMIDIFICATION The reduction of the relative humidity of the atmosphere by the use of chemical or mechanical methods.

DEGAUSSING The process of removing the magnetism from a magnetically recorded tape, thus erasing its contents.

DENSITY 1. The degree of optical opacity of a material, which determines the amount of light that will pass through it or reflect from it.
2. In DATA PROCESSING, the number of bits that can be stored per unit of dimension of a MEDIUM. In the case of MAGNETIC TAPE, this is expressed as bits per inch (bpi).

DEPOSIT 1. The placing of DOCUMENTS in the CUSTODY of an ARCHIVES (3) or MANUSCRIPT REPOSITORY without transfer of legal title.
2. The DOCUMENTS covered by such an action. *See also:* ACQUISITION

Depository *See:* REPOSITORY

DEPTH INDEXING The indexing of each specific subject contained in the text of a DOCUMENT, as contrasted with using relatively fewer general ACCESS POINTS.

DEPTH OF DESCRIPTION The amount of detailed information provided in a FINDING AID about the described materials in each ENTRY (2). Depth of description is also known as fullness. *See also:* LEVEL OF DESCRIPTION

DESCRIPTION 1. The process of analyzing, organizing, and recording information that serves to identify, manage, locate, and explain the HOLDINGS of ARCHIVES (3) and MANUSCRIPT REPOSITORIES and the CONTEXTS and records systems from which those HOLDINGS were selected.
2. The written representations or products of the above process.
3. In RECORDS MANAGEMENT, a written account of the physical characteristics, informational

CONTENT, and functional purpose of a record SE-RIES or system. (FRMGLOSS)

Descriptive Inventory *See:* INVENTORY

DESCRIPTIVE RECORD A representation of a UNIT OF DESCRIPTION.

DESCRIPTIVE STANDARD A rule or specification that guides DESCRIPTION.

Descriptive Unit *See:* UNIT OF DESCRIPTION

DESTRUCTION The disposal of DOCUMENTS of no further value by incineration, MACERATION, pulping, or SHREDDING. (ICA) *See also:* DISPOSITION

Destruction Schedule *See:* RECORDS SCHEDULE

DIARY A DOCUMENT containing the daily, personal accounts of the writer's own experiences, attitudes, and observations. *See also:* JOURNAL

DIAZO FILM A type of FILM used in duplicating MICROFILM in which an IMAGE is produced by the effect of light on diazonium-sensitized materials. It usually produces an IMAGE having the same POLARITY as the FILM from which it is duplicated. (Diazo film is not considered to be of ARCHIVAL QUALITY and is generally used for research copies rather than preservation copies.) *See also:* SILVER GELATIN FILM; VESICULAR FILM

DICTIONARY ARRANGEMENT A single alphabetical filing arrangement in which all types of EN-TRIES (2) (names, subjects, titles, etc.) are interfiled. *See also:* ENCYCLOPEDIC ARRANGEMENT

DIPLOMATICS The discipline that studies the genesis, FORMS (2), and transmission of archival DOCU-MENTS and their relationship with the facts represented in them and with their CREATOR, in order to identify, evaluate, and communicate their true nature.

DIRECT ACCESS 1. A method of retrieval that permits location of an ITEM or FILE without reference to an INDEX or other FINDING AID.
2. In computer-based information storage and RETRIEVAL (2), a method of referring to RECORDS (2) arranged in nonsequential order in a FILE (3). Access time to RECORDS (2) is not related to their location in the FILE (3), because all those preceding a desired one are ignored. Direct access is used synonymously with random access. (ALA) *See also:* INDIRECT ACCESS

DIRECT ENTRY An index ENTRY (2) that is in natural word order (as opposed to inverted order). *See also:* COMPLEX ENTRY; INVERTED ENTRY

DIRECTIVES MANAGEMENT The application of RECORDS MANAGEMENT principles and techniques to general instructions, orders, or other official issuances. (ICA)

DIRECTORY A compilation of names, addresses, and other data about specific groups of persons or organizations.

DISASTER PLAN The policies and procedures intended to prevent or minimize damage to archival materials resulting from disasters. *See also:* VITAL RECORDS MANAGEMENT

Disinfection *See:* FUMIGATION

Disinfestation *See:* FUMIGATION

Diskette *See:* FLOPPY DISK

DISPERSAL A process for safeguarding RECORDS in which copies are transferred to locations other than those where the originals are housed. *See also:* REMOTE STORAGE

DISPLAY CASE Protective equipment with transparent surfaces for exhibiting DOCUMENTS. Such equipment is also called an exhibition case or showcase.

Disposable Records *See:* TEMPORARY RECORDS

Disposal *See:* DISPOSITION

Disposal Date *See:* DISPOSITION DATE

DISPOSAL MICROFILMING The creation of MICRO-FILM to save or recover storage space and equipment and the substitution of the MICROFILM for the originals, which are destroyed. Disposal microfilming is also called space saving or substitution microfilming. (ICA) *See also:* ACQUISITION MICROFILM; PRESERVATION MICROFILMING; SECU-RITY MICROFILMING

Disposal Schedule *See:* RECORDS SCHEDULE

DISPOSITION The actions taken with regard to NON-CURRENT RECORDS as determined by their AP-PRAISAL pursuant to legislation, regulation, or administrative procedure. Actions include TRANSFER to an ARCHIVES (3) or DESTRUCTION.

DISPOSITION DATE The date specified in a RECORDS SCHEDULE on which a group of RECORDS is subject to DISPOSITION.

Disposition Schedule *See:* RECORDS SCHEDULE

DIVIDED CATALOG ARRANGEMENT An arrangement of a CATALOG in which ENTRIES (2) are separated into two or more sequences, such as author, subject, and title.

DOCKET A list or REGISTER of cases before a tribunal, usually kept by the clerk of the court, identifying the cases, with entries of action taken. The term, used originally in connection with judicial proceedings, is now also used in connection with quasi-judicial or administrative proceedings. (AAT)

DOCUMENT 1. Recorded information regardless of MEDIUM or characteristics.
2. A single ITEM.

Document Type *See:* FORM (2)

DOCUMENTARY EDITING The selection, description, and critical annotation of ORIGINAL DOCUMENTS for publication. Documentary editing is frequently called historical editing.

DOCUMENTARY PUBLICATION The publication of ORIGINAL DOCUMENTS with appropriate description and critical annotation.

DOCUMENTATION 1. In archival usage, the creation or acquisition of DOCUMENTS to provide evidence of the CREATOR, an event, or an activity. 2. In ELECTRONIC RECORDS, an organized series of descriptive DOCUMENTS explaining the operating system and software necessary to use and maintain a FILE (3) and the arrangement, CONTENT, and coding of the data which it contains. (ICA)

DOCUMENTATION STRATEGY An on-going, analytic, cooperative approach designed, promoted, and implemented by CREATORS, administrators (including ARCHIVISTS), and USERS to ensure the archival retention of appropriate DOCUMENTATION in some area of human endeavor through the application of archival techniques, the creation of institutional ARCHIVES (3) and redefined ACQUISITION POLICIES, and the development of sufficient resources. The key elements in this approach are an analysis of the universe to be documented, an understanding of the inherent documentary problems, and the formulation of a plan to assure the adequate DOCUMENTATION of an issue, activity, or geographic area.

Donation *See:* GIFT

DONOR A person or organization who has given DOCUMENTS to an ARCHIVES (3) or MANUSCRIPT REPOSITORY. *See also:* CREATOR; OFFICE OF ORIGIN; TRANSFERRING AGENCY

Donor Restriction *See:* RESTRICTED ACCESS

Dossier *See:* CASE FILE

DOUBLE LOOK-UP INDEX An INDEX using a locator or reference system which requires the user to consult another listing before finding the actual location of the information, concept, or data. (ARMA)

DOUBLE SHELVING The placing of ITEMS or containers behind each other on the same SHELF. (ICA)

DOWNGRADE To reduce the level of SECURITY CLASSIFICATION of specified information/RECORDS. (ICA) *See also:* DECLASSIFICATION

DRAFT 1. A rough or preliminary form of a DOCUMENT, sometimes retained as evidence. (ICA) 2. A written order directing the payment of money. (ICA)

DRAWING A representation of the appearance of material objects by means of lines and marks upon PAPER or another MEDIUM.

DRY SILVER PROCESS A non-gelatin silver copying process in which the latent IMAGE is made visible by the application of heat rather than of chemicals.

Dummy *See:* OUT-GUIDE

Duplicate *See:* COPY

DUPLICATE ORIGINAL 1. A COPY of a DOCUMENT, as complete as the original in all essential respects, including relevant SIGNATURES, if any. 2. A COPY, usually a signed LETTER, dispatched by an alternate route or by another means in an effort to ensure that the information contained therein will reach the addressee.

Duplicating Master *See:* MASTER

DURABILITY The degree to which a MEDIUM such as PAPER retains its original strength or properties, especially under conditions of heavy, sustained use. *See also:* PERMANENCE; PERMANENT/DURABLE PAPER

Electronic Data Processing (EDP) *See:* DATA PROCESSING

ELECTRONIC RECORDS RECORDS on electronic storage media. *See also:* MACHINE-READABLE RECORDS/ARCHIVES

ELECTROSTATIC PROCESS A direct, dry reproduction process creating COPIES on ordinary PAPER in an automatic machine using electrical photoconductivity. (ICA)

EMULSION A coating containing light-sensitive materials that creates a latent IMAGE upon EXPOSURE.

ENCAPSULATION The encasing of a DOCUMENT in a clear plastic (usually polyester) envelope of which the edges are sealed. The aim is to provide nonreactive support and protection for a fragile DOCUMENT and still maintain complete visibility. Encapsulation is normally preceded by DEACIDIFICATION.

ENCYCLOPEDIC ARRANGEMENT A method of filing in which broad major HEADINGS (2) are arranged in alphabetical order, with minor or subsidiary topics arranged alphabetically under the major HEADING (2) to which they relate. (ARMA) *See also:* DICTIONARY ARRANGEMENT

ENDORSEMENT A NOTE, title, SIGNATURE, etc. written on the back of a DOCUMENT. (ICA)

Enduring Value *See:* ARCHIVAL VALUE

ENGROSSED COPY The final version of an official DOCUMENT, drawn up in accordance with prescribed form.

ENGROSSMENT 1. The preparation of an ENGROSSED COPY. (ICA)
2. An ENGROSSED COPY. (ICA)

ENLARGEMENT A REPRODUCTION larger than the original or the intermediate used to make the REPRODUCTION. (ICA)

Enlargement Ratio *See:* MAGNIFICATION

ENLARGER-PRINTER An optical device for producing ENLARGEMENTS, incorporating processing facilities for the rapid production of HARD COPY, usually under conditions of room lighting. (ICA)

Entrance Interview *See:* REFERENCE INTERVIEW

ENTRY 1. The recording of a DOCUMENT, TRANSACTION, or other information in a CATALOG, JOURNAL, list, REGISTER, etc.
2. An item thus recorded.
3. The UNIT OF DESCRIPTION in a FINDING AID or RECORDS SCHEDULE.

ENVIRONMENTAL CONTROL The creation and maintenance of a storage environment for archival HOLDINGS conducive to their long-term preservation. Environmental control encompasses temperature, relative humidity, air quality, lighting, freedom from biological infestation, housekeeping procedures, SECURITY, and protection from fire and water damage.

EPHEMERA DOCUMENTS created specifically for a transitory purpose. Advertisements, calling cards, notices, and tickets are examples of ephemera.

Essential Record *See:* VITAL RECORD

Estate Archives *See:* FAMILY (AND ESTATE) ARCHIVES

ESTRAY A DOCUMENT not in the possession of its legal custodian. (ICA) *See also:* ALIENATION (2); REMOVED ARCHIVES; REPLEVIN

Estreat *See:* EXTRACT

Evaluation *See:* APPRAISAL

EVIDENTIAL VALUE The worth of DOCUMENTS/ARCHIVES for illuminating the nature and work of their CREATOR by providing evidence of the CREATOR'S origins, FUNCTIONS, and activities. Evidential value is distinct from informational value. *See also:* ADMINISTRATIVE VALUE; FISCAL VALUE; INFORMATIONAL VALUE; INTRINSIC VALUE; LEGAL VALUE

Exhibit *See:* EXHIBITION

EXHIBITION The display of ORIGINAL DOCUMENTS or copies thereof for educational and cultural purposes. (ICA)

Exhibition Case *See:* DISPLAY CASE

Exit Interview *See:* REFERENCE INTERVIEW

EXPOSURE 1. The process of submitting light-sensitive materials to a light source for a predetermined time period in order to produce a latent IMAGE. (ALA)
2. A section of FILM which has been subjected to a light source. (ALA)

EXTRACT A COPY of part of the text of a DOCUMENT. (ICA) *See also:* ABSTRACT

FACETED CLASSIFICATION A scheme of CLASSIFICATION in which terms are grouped by conceptual categories and ordered so as to display their generic relationships. (ICA)

Facilitative Records *See:* ADMINISTRATIVE RECORDS

FACSIMILE 1. A REPRODUCTION of a DOCUMENT that approximates as nearly as possible the CONTENT, FORM (2), and appearance of the original, but not necessarily the size.
2. The exact IMAGE of a DOCUMENT transmitted electronically to another location. Used in this context, a facsimile is often referred to as a "fax."

FAIR COPY An exact COPY of a DOCUMENT incorporating all final textual corrections and revisions. (ICA)

FAIR USE A concept in COPYRIGHT law that provides for certain exceptions to the exclusive rights of COPYRIGHT owners in cases relating to teaching, research, scholarship, and news reporting.

FALSE DROP In an automated retrieval system, information retrieved that does not pertain to the subject sought. *See also:* HIT

FAMILY (AND ESTATE) ARCHIVES RECORDS/ARCHIVES of one or more related families and/or the individual members thereof relating to their private and public affairs and to the administration of their estates. (ICA)

Fax *See:* FACSIMILE (2)

Fiche *See:* MICROFICHE

FIELD A specific area of a computer RECORD (2) allocated for a particular category of data, usually one DATA ELEMENT. In some applications, each field is assigned a fixed number of positions (fixed-length fields); in other applications, each field may vary within defined limits (variable-length fields). Fields that must be present in every RECORD (2) are known as required fields; fields that may or may not be present in every RECORD (2) are known as variable-occurrence fields.

FIELD-TAG An alpha-numerical code used to identify a FIELD.

FILE 1. An organized unit (folder, volume, etc.) of DOCUMENTS grouped together either for current use or in the process of archival ARRANGEMENT. (ICA)

2. A series of FILES (1). (ICA)

3. In DATA PROCESSING, two or more RECORDS (2) of identical layout treated as a unit. The unit is larger than a RECORD (2) but smaller than a data system, and is also known as a data set or file set.

4. Storage equipment, such as a filing cabinet.

FILE BREAK A convenient point within a FILING PLAN/SYSTEM (end of a letter of the alphabet, end of year or month, etc.) at which FILES are separated for purposes of storage and/or DISPOSITION.

File Classification Scheme *See:* CLASSIFICATION PLAN/SCHEME

File Copy *See:* RECORD COPY

File Cover *See:* FOLDER

FILE GUIDE A divider with a projecting TAB used to identify sections of a FILE (2).

FILE INTEGRITY The concept that the accuracy, completeness, and original order of the RECORDS in a FILING SYSTEM must be maintained. *See also:* ARCHIVAL INTEGRITY

FILE MAINTENANCE 1. The activity of keeping a FILE (3) up to date by adding, changing, or deleting data. (UN)

2. The systematic inspection of a FILE (2) for the purposes of replacing worn file FOLDERS, mending torn DOCUMENTS, removing duplicate COPIES, locating possible misfiles, and insuring proper sequence of contents.

File Set *See:* FILE (3)

File Unit *See:* FILE

FILES A collective term frequently applied to part or all of the RECORDS of an office or an AGENCY.

FILES ADMINISTRATION/MANAGEMENT The application of RECORDS MANAGEMENT techniques to filing practices, in order to maintain RECORDS easily and to retrieve them rapidly, to ensure their completeness, and to facilitate the DISPOSITION of NONCURRENT RECORDS.

FILING PLAN A CLASSIFICATION PLAN/SCHEME for the physical arrangement, storage, and RETRIEVAL of FILES. A filing plan is usually identified by the type of symbols used (e.g. alphabetical, numerical, alpha-numerical, decimal). *See also:* STANDARDIZED FILING PLAN/SYSTEM

FILING SYSTEM A group of conventions, methods, and procedural rules according to which DOCUMENTS are sorted, classified, cross-referenced, stored, and retrieved.

FILM A flexible sheet or strip of transparent plastic upon which IMAGES can be recorded. (ICA) *See also:* MICROFILM

Film Frame *See:* FRAME

Film Jacket *See:* MICROFILM JACKET

FILM FOOTAGE A general term used to measure or describe FILM or video sequences. This term derives from the fact that amounts of FILM are measured in feet, and the term has migrated to television/video (where the standard of measurement is in minutes and seconds or in FRAMES).

FILM RECORDS/ARCHIVES RECORDS/ARCHIVES in the form of MOTION PICTURES. *See also:* AUDIO-VISUAL RECORDS/ARCHIVES

FILMSTRIP A short length of FILM carrying a number of photographic IMAGES, each intended to be viewed separately.

FINDING AID The descriptive tool, published or unpublished, manual or electronic, produced by a CREATOR, RECORDS CENTER, ARCHIVES (3), or MANUSCRIPT REPOSITORY to establish PHYSICAL CONTROL and/or INTELLECTUAL CONTROL over RECORDS and/or archival materials. Basic finding aids include local, regional, or national descriptive databases; GUIDES; INVENTORIES; REGISTERS (2); location registers; CATALOGS; SPECIAL LISTS; shelf and CONTAINER LISTS; INDEXES; CALENDAR and, for ELECTRONIC RECORDS, software DOCUMENTATION (2).

FIRE DETECTION SYSTEM A system for detecting the outbreak of a fire in its earliest stages by means of electronic detectors activated by smoke, rise in temperature, or by changes in the ionization of the atmosphere.

FIRE EXTINGUISHING SYSTEM A system for extinguishing a fire by manual or automatic means. Manual extinguishing systems may use water, foam, sand, or powder; automatic systems may use water, gas, or, rarely, foam.

FISCAL VALUE The worth of RECORDS/ARCHIVES for the conduct of current or future financial or fiscal business and/or as evidence thereof. *See also:* ADMINISTRATIVE VALUE; LEGAL VALUE

Fixed-Length Field *See:* FIELD

Flat-Bed Camera *See:* PLANETARY CAMERA

FLAT-FILING The storage of DOCUMENTS, whether bound or in containers, in a position parallel to the SHELF. Flat-filing is also called horizontal filing. *See also:* VERTICAL FILING

FLATTENING The process of restoring to a flat condition DOCUMENTS that have been folded, rolled, or are otherwise in need of such treatment, usually by the application of pressure which has been preceded by HUMIDIFICATION.

FLOOR LOAD The capacity of a floor area to support a given weight expressed in terms of weight per unit of area. (ARMA)

FLOOR-SPACE RATIO The ratio of volume capacity to area of floor space required to store RECORDS. (ARMA)

FLOPPY DISK A flexible MAGNETIC DISK revolving within a protective cover. A floppy disk is also called a diskette. *See also:* HARD DISK

FOLDER A folded sheet of cardboard or heavy PAPER serving as a container for a number of DOCUMENTS.

FOLDER LIST A list prepared by the CREATOR or an ARCHIVES (3) or MANUSCRIPT REPOSITORY detailing the titles of FOLDERS contained in one or more RECORDS CENTER CARTONS/CONTAINERS or ARCHIVES BOXES/CONTAINERS. *See also:* CONTAINER LIST

FOLIATION 1. The act of numbering the leaves or FOLIOS of a DOCUMENT as distinct from numbering PAGES, i.e., pagination.
2. The result of this action. (ICA)

FOLIO 1. A LEAF of PAPER or PARCHMENT usually folded and numbered only on the front. (ICA)
2. The number assigned to a LEAF. (ICA)
3. A VOLUME made up of SHEETS folded once; hence, loosely, a VOLUME of large dimensions. (ICA)

FOLLOW-UP INTERVIEW An interviewing technique, employed at any time following the use of materials by RESEARCHERS, to evaluate their satisfaction with materials used and services provided by the ARCHIVES (3) or MANUSCRIPT REPOSITORY. The follow-up interview may be oral or written. *See also:* REFERENCE INTERVIEW; USE/USER STUDY

FONDS The whole of the DOCUMENTS, regardless of FORM (2) or MEDIUM, organically created and/or accumulated and used by a particular person, family, or CORPORATE BODY in the conduct of per-

sonal or corporate activity. (AHCDS) *See also:* MANUSCRIPT GROUP; RECORD GROUP

Footage *See:* FILM FOOTAGE

FORGERY A DOCUMENT falsified wholly or in part in CONTENT or FORM (2) with intention to deceive through its acceptance as an original. (ICA)

FORM 1. A DOCUMENT, printed or otherwise produced, with predesignated recording of specified information.
2. In DIPLOMATICS, all the characteristics of a DOCUMENT that can be separated from its CONTENT. It can be distinguished as physical or intellectual. Physical form is the external make-up of a DOCUMENT; intellectual form is its internal articulations, the arrangement of its parts. *See also:* GENRE; MEDIUM; RECORD TYPE

Form of Material *See:* FORM (2)

FORMAT 1. The plan or arrangement of a DOCUMENT.
2. In DATA PROCESSING, the arrangement of data.
3. In descriptive practice, a selection of descriptive elements arranged in a prescribed manner and sequence so that the resulting DESCRIPTION (2) will be standardized.

FORMS MANAGEMENT The application of RECORDS MANAGEMENT principles and techniques to the analysis, design, construction, production, logistics, maintenance, and use of FORMS to provide improved quality, increased efficiency, and reduced costs.

FORMULA A set form of words or a prescribed statement, used in official DOCUMENTS, in which a general fact, rule, or principle is defined or declared. Formulas may be prescribed by authority or custom.

FORMULARY A VOLUME containing a collection or system of stated and prescribed FORMS and/or FORMULAS to be used as models (e.g., OATHS, declarations, CONTRACTS, etc.).

FOXING The discoloration of PAPER by brownish stains, often in the form of specks or small spots.

FRAME The area of a photographic FILM exposed to light in a camera during one EXPOSURE. (ICA)

Freeze Drying *See:* VACUUM FREEZE DRYING

FREQUENCY COUNT The total number of occurrences of individual words or other elements in a body of data.

FROZEN RECORDS In RECORDS MANAGEMENT, those TEMPORARY RECORDS that cannot be destroyed on schedule because special circumstances, such as a court order, require a temporary extension of the approved RETENTION PERIOD. (FRMGLOSS) *See also:* HOLD ORDER

Fugitive Archives *See:* REMOVED ARCHIVES

Fullness *See:* DEPTH OF DESCRIPTION

FUMIGATION The process of exposing DOCUMENTS, usually in a vacuum or other airtight chamber, to gas or vapor to destroy insects or mold. Fumigation is also referred to as disinfection or disinfestation.

FUMIGATION CHAMBER A vacuum or other airtight chamber used for the FUMIGATION of DOCUMENTS. (ICA)

FUNCTION An activity directed at carrying out a mission for an organization. For example, functions of an ARCHIVES (3) include such activities as APPRAISAL, ARRANGEMENT, and REFERENCE SERVICE. *See also:* COMPETENCE; MANDATE

Functional Arrangement *See:* ARRANGEMENT

FUNCTIONAL PERTINENCE The relationship of a group of DOCUMENTS to one FUNCTION. For example, teaching notes pertain to the FUNCTION of education. The concept is used in making appraisal determinations.

FUNCTIONAL PROVENANCE The origin of a group of DOCUMENTS with respect to the FUNCTION that produced them, rather than the CREATOR. The concept allows for the establishment and maintenance of INTELLECTUAL CONTROL on multi-provenance SERIES resulting from administrative and/or political change. The concept ensures that, with a transfer of FUNCTIONS from one authority to another, relevant RECORDS or copies thereof are also transferred to ensure administrative continuity. *See also:* PROVENANCE

FUNCTIONAL SOVEREIGNTY (PRINCIPLE OF) A principle originally formulated in Australia as a response to administrative change and to the consequent existence of multi-provenance SERIES. According to the principle, when accessioning and describing a multi-provenance SERIES of RECORDS, it is necessary to identify its links not only with the creating agency, but also with the CONTROLLING AGENCY, that is, with the AGENCY that may have succeeded to the relevant FUNCTIONS of the CREATOR(S). Functional sovereignty is an extension of the principle of PROVENANCE. *See also:* OFFICE OF ORIGIN; TRANSFERRING AGENCY; SERIES DESCRIPTIVE SYSTEM

Gaseous Fire Suppression System *See:* FIRE EXTINGUISHING SYSTEM

General Guide *See:* GUIDE

GENERAL INDEX An INDEX giving ACCESS to one or more bodies of material or to the totality of HOLDINGS of a RECORDS CENTER, ARCHIVES (2), or MANUSCRIPT REPOSITORY.

GENERAL RECORD GROUP A RECORD GROUP usually comprising the RECORDS of the office of the head of an organizationally complex AGENCY and frequently other RECORDS of units of the AGENCY concerned with matters common to the entire AGENCY, such as fiscal or personnel matters. A general record group is a practical modification of the RECORD GROUP concept. *See also:* COLLECTIVE RECORD GROUP

GENERAL RECORDS SCHEDULE A RECORDS SCHEDULE governing specified SERIES of RECORDS common to several or all AGENCIES or administrative units of a CORPORATE BODY. A general records schedule is also called a common records schedule or general schedule.

General Schedule *See:* GENERAL RECORDS SCHEDULE

GENERATION The degree of remoteness of a COPY, usually photographic, from the original. (ICA)

GENRE A distinctive type or category of artistic or literary composition characterized by a particular style, FORM (2), and/or CONTENT (e.g., comedy, documentary, essay, or hymn). *See also:* RECORD TYPE

Geographical Arrangement *See:* ARRANGEMENT

GIFT An addition to HOLDINGS acquired without monetary consideration and becoming the sole property of the recipient, frequently effected by a DEED OF GIFT.

GO LIST A list of words that are allowed as index terms in an automated INDEX. Incorporated into a computerized system, index references will be generated wherever these terms appear. *See also:* STOP LIST

GOVERNMENT DOCUMENT/PUBLICATION Any publication originating in, or issued with the imprint of, or at the expense and by the authority of, any office of a legally organized governmental organization. *See also:* PRINTED ARCHIVES

Grant, Land *See:* LAND GRANT

GUIDE 1. A FINDING AID giving a general account of all or part of the HOLDINGS of one or several ARCHIVES (2) and/or MANUSCRIPT REPOSITORIES. A guide is usually arranged by COLLECTION (1,2), FONDS, or RECORD GROUP.

2. A FINDING AID describing the HOLDINGS of one or more ARCHIVES (2) and/or MANUSCRIPT REPOSITORIES relating to particular subjects, periods, or geographical areas or to specified types or

categories of DOCUMENTS. This type of guide is usually called a thematic or subject guide. *See also:* FILE GUIDE; SUMMARY GUIDE

Hand Lamination *See:* LAMINATION

HARD COPY A DOCUMENT, usually on PAPER, that can be read with the unaided eye, as opposed to a MICROFORM or ELECTRONIC RECORD.

HARD DISK A hardware device used to store electronic data. It is not flexible (unlike a FLOPPY DISK) and is completely enclosed in an airtight case to exclude dust. *See also:* FLOPPY DISK

HEADING 1. The title or inscription at the head of a PAGE, chapter, or other section of a DOCUMENT. 2. A name, word, or phrase at the beginning of an ENTRY (2) in an INDEX, CATALOG, or other FINDING AID, which serves as an ACCESS POINT to the materials being described.

HIERARCHICAL DESCRIPTIVE SYSTEM Any archival descriptive system in which materials are described at various levels ranging on a continuum from the largest aggregate level (RECORD GROUP, FONDS, or COLLECTION (1,2)) to intermediate levels (SUBGROUP, SERIES, SUBSERIES, FILE) to the smallest unit (ITEM). *See also:* LEVEL OF DESCRIPTION; MULTILEVEL DESCRIPTION; SERIES DESCRIPTIVE SYSTEM

Historical Editing *See:* DOCUMENTARY EDITING

Historical Manuscripts *See:* MANUSCRIPTS

HIT In an automated retrieval system, a term used to represent information located by the system that appears to meet or match search specifications. *See also:* FALSE DROP

HOLD ORDER A written or verbal order directing that a RECORD or SERIES be retained beyond the established RETENTION PERIOD because of extenuating circumstances. *See also:* FROZEN RECORDS

HOLDING AREA An area used for temporary storage of RECORDS.

HOLDINGS The totality of DOCUMENTS in the CUSTODY of a RECORDS CENTER, ARCHIVES (3), or MANUSCRIPT REPOSITORY.

HOLDINGS MAINTENANCE A PRESERVATION activity that includes unfolding or unrolling DOCUMENTS, removing or replacing harmful fasteners, reproducing unstable DOCUMENTS, placing mate-

rials in acid-free FOLDERS and boxes, and shelving them in environmentally controlled and secure storage.

Hollinger Box (TM) *See:* ARCHIVES BOX/CONTAINER

HOLOGRAPH A DOCUMENT entirely in the handwriting of the person who signed it. (ICA) *See also:* AUTOGRAPH (2)

HONEYCOMBING The process of leaving space between shelved RECORDS in stack areas for future ACCESSIONS (2) or ACCRUALS to RECORD GROUPS, FONDS, or COLLECTIONS (1,2), SUBGROUPS, or SERIES already accessioned in part.

Horizontal Filing *See:* FLAT-FILING

Housekeeping Records *See:* ADMINISTRATIVE RECORDS

HUMIDIFICATION 1. The placing of DOCUMENTS in moisture-laden air, in a cloud chamber or container, to aid in the gradual absorption of water vapor to restore pliability.
2. The increase of relative humidity in an archival storage area. *See also:* FLATTENING

HYGROMETER An instrument for measuring relative humidity. (ICA)

HYGROTHERMOGRAPH A device used to measure and record both relative humidity and temperature. *See also:* THERMOHYGROMETER

ICONOGRAPHIC RECORDS/ARCHIVES RECORDS/ ARCHIVES in the form of pictures, PHOTOGRAPHS, illustrations, PRINTS (2), and the products of other pictorial processes. *See also:* PHOTOGRAPHIC RECORDS/ARCHIVES

ILLUMINATED MANUSCRIPT A MANUSCRIPT whose text or initial letters are decorated with ornamental designs, miniature DRAWINGS, or paintings through the use of colors or precious metals. An illuminated manuscript is also called an illumination.

Illumination *See:* ILLUMINATED MANUSCRIPT

IMAGE A REPRODUCTION of the subject matter copied, usually by photography. (ICA)

IMPRESCRIPTIBILITY The concept that because PUBLIC RECORDS/ARCHIVES are inalienable public property, they remain permanently subject to REPLEVIN. *See also:* INALIENABILITY

Inactive Records *See:* NONCURRENT RECORDS

INALIENABILITY The quality of PUBLIC RECORDS/ARCHIVES that prevents such materials from being alienated, surrendered, or transferred to anybody not entitled by law to their ownership. This concept is also called inviolability. *See also:* IMPRESCRIPTIBILITY

INCLUSIVE DATES The beginning and ending dates of the materials being described. *See also:* BULK DATES

Indefinite Value *See:* ARCHIVAL VALUE

INDENTURE An INSTRUMENT to which two or more persons are parties, and in which the parties enter into reciprocal and corresponding grants or obligations toward each other. The term derives from the practice of making as many copies of the DEED as there were parties, and cutting or indenting each COPY (either in acute angles, like the teeth of a saw, or in a waving line) at the top or side, the idea being that the genuineness of each part might be proved by its fitting into the indentations cut in the other.

INDEX A systematically arranged list providing ACCESS to the contents of a FILE (2), DOCUMENT, or groups of DOCUMENTS, consisting of ENTRIES (2) giving enough information to trace or locate each ENTRY (2) by means of a page number or other symbol.

Index, General *See:* GENERAL INDEX

Index Language *See:* INDEX VOCABULARY

INDEX VOCABULARY The set of terms to be used in indexing the CONTENTS of DOCUMENTS in an INFORMATION RETRIEVAL SYSTEM. Index vocabulary is synonymous with index language. *See also:* LEAD-IN VOCABULARY

INDICTMENT A formal written accusation originating with a prosecutor and issued by a grand jury against a party charged with a crime. (AAT)

INDIRECT ACCESS A method of locating information requiring prior use of an INDEX. (ARMA) *See also:* DIRECT ACCESS

INFORMATICS The study of the structure and properties of information, as well as the application of technology to the organization, storage, retrieval, and dissemination of information. (ALA) *See also:* INFORMATION SCIENCE

INFORMATION MANAGEMENT The administration of information, its use and transmission, and the application of theories and techniques of INFORMATION SCIENCE to create, modify, or improve information handling systems.

Information Processing *See:* DATA PROCESSING

INFORMATION RESOURCES MANAGEMENT (IRM) A managerial discipline that views information as a resource analogous to financial, physical, human, and natural resources, and stresses the efficient and effective handling of information. *See also:* DATA PROCESSING; RECORDS MANAGEMENT

INFORMATION RETRIEVAL SYSTEM A set of procedures, usually automated, by which references to or the data contained in DOCUMENTS are indexed and stored in such a matter that they can be retrieved in response to specific requests. (ICA)

INFORMATION SCIENCE The study of the theory and practice relating to the creation, acquisition, processing, management, retrieval, and dissemination of information. *See also:* INFORMATICS

INFORMATION SYSTEM The organized collection, processing, transmission, and dissemination of information in accordance with defined procedures.

INFORMATIONAL VALUE The worth of DOCUMENTS/ARCHIVES for reference and research deriving from the information they contain on persons, places, subjects, etc., as distinct from their EVIDENTIAL VALUE. *See also:* ADMINISTRATIVE VALUE; INTRINSIC VALUE

Initial Interview *See:* REFERENCE INTERVIEW

INJUNCTION An order issued by a court of equity enjoining or prohibiting a party from doing some specified act.

INSPECTION (RIGHT OF) The legally imposed responsibility of an ARCHIVES (3) or a RECORDS MANAGEMENT program to inspect and propose measures to improve the RECORDS creation, maintenance, and DISPOSITION practices of operating AGENCIES within its jurisdiction.

INSTRUMENT A DOCUMENT, such as a CONTRACT or DEED, executed and delivered as formal evidence of a legal act or agreement, for the purpose of creating, securing, modifying, or terminating a right.

Instrument of Gift *See:* DEED OF GIFT

INTELLECTUAL CONTROL The acquisition and creation of DOCUMENTATION required to access the informational CONTENT of RECORDS. (UN) *See also:* ADMINISTRATIVE CONTROL; PHYSICAL CONTROL

Intellectual Form *See:* FORM (2)

Intellectual Property *See:* COPYRIGHT

INTERFILE The process of placing RECORDS in their proper sequence within an existing system.

INTERLEAVING The placing of sheets of one material between sheets of a similar or different material for such purposes as drying wet DOCUMENTS, providing an alkaline buffer, or preventing DOCUMENTS from rubbing.

Inter-Relationship *See:* ARCHIVAL NATURE

Inter-Repository Guide *See:* GUIDE

INTRINSIC VALUE The inherent worth of a DOCU-MENT based upon factors such as age, CONTENT, usage, circumstances of creation, SIGNATURE, or attached SEALS (2). *See also:* ADMINISTRATIVE VALUE; EVIDENTIAL VALUE; INFORMATIONAL VALUE

INVENTORY 1. A basic archival FINDING AID whose unit of ENTRY (3) is usually the SERIES. An inventory generally includes a brief ADMINISTRATIVE HISTORY of the organization(s) whose RECORDS are being described as well as DESCRIPTIONS (2) of the RECORDS. SERIES DESCRIPTIONS give as a minimum such data as title, INCLUSIVE DATES, quantity, arrangement, relationships to other SE-RIES, and SCOPE AND CONTENT NOTES. Inventories may also contain appendices that provide such supplementary information as CONTAINER LISTS, FOLDER LISTS, a glossary of abbreviations and special terms, lists of file units on special subjects, INDEXES, and CLASSIFICATION PLANS/SCHEMES. 2. In RECORDS MANAGEMENT, a detailed listing of the VOLUME (2), scope, and complexity of an organization's RECORDS, usually compiled for the purpose of creating a RECORDS SCHEDULE.

INVERTED ENTRY An index ENTRY (2) with the normal order of words transposed to bring a particular word into prominence as the filing element. For example, "Description, Archival" is an IN-VERTED ENTRY. *See also:* COMPLEX ENTRY; DIRECT ENTRY

Inviolability *See:* INALIENABILITY

IRM *See:* INFORMATION RESOURCES MANAGEMENT (IRM)

ITEM The smallest indivisible archival unit (e.g., a LETTER, MEMORANDUM, REPORT, leaflet, or PHOTO-GRAPH). Items accumulate to form SERIES. *See also:* DOCUMENT; RECORD

Jacket, Microfilm *See:* MICROFILM JACKET

JOURNAL 1. A chronological RECORD containing impersonal accounts of an individual's or organization's daily occurrences or TRANSACTIONS or of the proceedings of a legislative or other body.

2. In double-entry bookkeeping, an ACCOUNT BOOK into which are transcribed the items entered in the DAY BOOK. Journals are organized by account and make for more convenient posting in the LEDGER than do DAY BOOKS, which are organized by order of TRANSACTION.

JUDGMENT The official and authentic decision of a court of justice upon the respective rights and claims of the parties to an action or suit.

KEYWORD A word or group of words taken from the title or text of a DOCUMENT characterizing its CONTENT and facilitating its RETRIEVAL. (ICA) *See also:* THESAURUS

KEYWORD AND CONTEXT (KWAC) INDEX An INDEX of titles of DOCUMENTS permuted to bring each significant word to the beginning, in alphabetical order, followed by the remaining words that follow it in the title, and then followed by that part of the original title that came before the significant word.

KEYWORD IN CONTEXT (KWIC) INDEX An INDEX of titles or of significant phrases from AB-STRACTS, with the KEYWORDS put in a fixed position within the title or sentence and arranged in alphabetical order in a column.

KEYWORD OUT OF CONTEXT (KWOC) INDEX An INDEX of titles or of significant sentences from ABSTRACTS, that are printed in full under as many KEYWORDS as considered useful; the KEY-WORDS are separated from the titles on separate lines of their own and act as subject HEADINGS (2).

KWAC Index *See:* KEYWORD AND CONTEXT (KWAC) INDEX

KWIC Index *See:* KEYWORD IN CONTEXT (KWIC) INDEX

KWOC Index *See:* KEYWORD OUT OF CONTEXT (KWOC) INDEX

LABELING The process of preparing and affixing labels to FOLDERS, other file units, and containers.

Ladder *See:* PULPIT LADDER

LAMINATION A process, preceded by DEACIDIFICA-TION, for reinforcing a weak or damaged paper DOCUMENT by enclosing it between two sheets of thin tissue. The methods of attaching the tissue are:

(a) thermoplastic lamination, which involves the application of heat and pressure to two sheets of plastic foil, usually cellulose acetate; or

(b) hand or solvent lamination, in which adhesion is created by placing a sheet of plastic foil, usually cellulose acetate, between the tissue and the DOCUMENT and applying acetone. *See also:* DEACIDIFICATION; SILKING

LAND GRANT An official DOCUMENT from a government to an individual conveying fee-simple title to public lands. (AAT)

LANTERN SLIDE A POSITIVE, transparent IMAGE on a glass slide for projection, originally, by magic lantern.

Laser Disc *See:* OPTICAL DISC

LATERAL FILE Equipment that stores RECORDS vertically from side to side rather than front to back. *See also:* VERTICAL FILE

LAW A DOCUMENT stating rules of action or conduct prescribed by controlling authority and having binding legal force. (AAT)

LEAD-IN VOCABULARY In an INDEX VOCABULARY, references from synonymous and quasi-synonymous terms to preferred terms to be used in indexing the CONTENTS of DOCUMENTS in an INFORMATION RETRIEVAL SYSTEM.

LEAF A SHEET of PAPER or PARCHMENT each side of which is referred to as a PAGE. (ICA)

LEDGER A DOCUMENT of final ENTRY in accounting in which are entered debits, credits, and all other money TRANSACTIONS under each individual account or HEADING.

Legal Custody *See:* CUSTODY

LEGAL SIZE 1. A standard paper size 8 1/2 x 14 inches.
2. Capable of holding LEGAL SIZE DOCUMENTS. *See also:* LETTER SIZE; METRIC SIZE

LEGAL VALUE The worth of RECORDS/ARCHIVES for the conduct of current or future legal business and/or as legal evidence thereof. *See also:* ADMINISTRATIVE VALUE; FISCAL VALUE

LETTER 1. A communication in writing from one person to another. It can be distinguished from other forms of written communication because it usually contains a salutation and the SIGNATURE of the author or the author's delegate.

2. An official DOCUMENT conferring specified powers or privileges. (ICA)

Letter Book *See:* LETTERBOOK

LETTER SIZE 1. A standard paper size 8 1/2 by 11 inches.
2. Capable of holding LETTER SIZE DOCUMENTS. *See also:* LEGAL SIZE; METRIC SIZE.

LETTERBOOK 1. A VOLUME of blank or lined PAGES on which LETTERS have been written. The LETTERS may be DRAFTS written by the author or FAIR COPIES made by the author or a clerk.
2. Copies of LETTERS, originally on loose SHEETS and most frequently CARBON COPIES, bound together, usually in chronological order. *See also:* LETTERPRESS COPYBOOK

LETTER-BY-LETTER ARRANGEMENT A method of filing in which words, names, or phrases are arranged in alphabetical order irrespective of word breaks or punctuation. *See also:* WORD-BY-WORD ARRANGEMENT

LETTERPRESS COPYBOOK A book of tissue papers in which DOCUMENTS (usually LETTERS sent) were copied by transfer of ink through direct contact with the original using moisture and pressure in a copy press. A COPY of a single DOCUMENT produced by this method is referred to as a letterpress copy or press copy. This copying method was frequently used between 1820 and 1920. *See also:* LETTERBOOK

LEVEL OF DESCRIPTION The level of arrangement chosen as the UNIT OF DESCRIPTION in a FINDING AID. *See also:* HIERARCHICAL DESCRIPTIVE SYSTEM

LEVELS OF ARRANGEMENT The hierarchical groupings of archival HOLDINGS for purposes of ADMINISTRATIVE CONTROL and INTELLECTUAL CONTROL. The levels are: REPOSITORY; RECORD GROUP, FONDS, or COLLECTION (1,2); SUBGROUP(S); SERIES; SUBSERIES; FILE; and ITEM.

LICENSE A DOCUMENT evidencing a right or permission, granted to an individual or organization in accordance with law by a competent authority to engage in some TRANSACTION, business, or occupation, or to do some act. (AAT)

LIFE CONTINUUM In Canada, the unified pattern of a RECORD's life, comprised of four interrelated stages: creation or receipt; CLASSIFICATION; SCHEDULING and its implementations, including maintenance in the creating office, an active storage area or RECORDS CENTER, or an ARCHIVES (2); and use (primary or secondary). *See also:* LIFE CYCLE (OF A RECORD)

LIFE CYCLE (OF A RECORD) The life span of a RECORD from its creation or receipt to its final DISPOSITION.

LIFE CYCLE TRACKING The control of RECORDS throughout their LIFE CYCLE. The control involves the identification, DESCRIPTION, and SCHEDULING of RECORDS from their creation, and the production of prompts or REPORTS to activate such actions as microfilming, TRANSFER to a RECORDS CENTER or ARCHIVES (2), VITAL RECORDS protective actions, and DESTRUCTION. The control can also extend to the monitoring of actions performed on RECORDS following their TRANSFER to a RECORDS CENTER or ARCHIVES (2). LIFE CYCLE TRACKING commonly, but not necessarily, employs the use of automated techniques and tools. *See also:* LIFE CONTINUUM

LINE CODE INDEX A visual INDEX, used on roll MICROFILM, where a stream of bars determines the general location of a particular DOCUMENT on the FILM. (ARMA)

LINEAR FEET 1. A measurement for descriptive and control purposes of shelf space occupied by DOCUMENTS. For vertical files (RECORDS filed on edge) the total length of drawers, shelves, or other equipment occupied is calculated; in the case of material filed horizontally (flat or piled up), the total vertical thickness is used. LINEAR FEET, except for card indexes and oversized materials, may be equated with CUBIC FEET on a one-to-one basis for DESCRIPTION of textual records. *See also:* CUBIC FEET

2. A measurement for descriptive and control purposes of the length of FILM, tape, or MICROFILM (usually expressed as feet). *See also:* FILM FOOTAGE

LITERARY MANUSCRIPTS DRAFTS, NOTES, worksheets, MANUSCRIPTS, proofs, and other production materials commonly associated with the creation of fiction, poetry, and other literary works. *See also:* PRODUCTION PAPERS

LOAN The temporary physical TRANSFER of archival materials to an outside location for reference or consultation, REPRODUCTION, or EXHIBITION purposes.

Local Records *See:* PUBLIC RECORDS

LOCATION INDEX/REGISTER A FINDING AID used to control and locate HOLDINGS. *See also:* SHELF LIST

LOGICAL RECORD In DATA PROCESSING, a RECORD (2) defined on the basis of its CONTENT, rather than its physical location or space requirements. *See also:* PHYSICAL RECORD

MACERATION The DESTRUCTION of DOCUMENTS by soaking them in liquid in order to decompose them. Maceration is also called pulping.

Machine-Indexing *See:* COMPUTER-BASED INDEXING

MACHINE-READABLE RECORDS/ARCHIVES RECORDS/ARCHIVES, usually in code, recorded on a MEDIUM such as a MAGNETIC DISK, MAGNETIC TAPE, or PUNCHED CARD/TAPE, whose contents are accessible only by machine and organized in accordance with the principle of PROVENANCE as distinct from DATA ARCHIVES. (ICA) *See also:* ELECTRONIC RECORDS

MAGNETIC DISK A flat circular MEDIUM, the surfaces of which are covered with a magnetized layer permitting the recording and storage of electronic data.

MAGNETIC MEDIA Various recording materials coated with magnetic material on which data can be stored by selective magnetization of portions of the surface, e.g., MAGNETIC TAPE or FLOPPY DISKS.

MAGNETIC TAPE A tape coated with a magnetizable material, capable of storing information in the form of electromagnetic signals. (ICA)

MAGNIFICATION The linear ratio of the size of an IMAGE to that of the ORIGINAL DOCUMENT when viewed through or projected by an optical instrument. Magnification is also referred to as enlargement ratio.

MAIL MANAGEMENT The application of RECORDS MANAGEMENT principles and techniques to the flow of mail. (ICA)

MAIN ENTRY The ACCESS POINT considered primary in a DESCRIPTIVE RECORD. *See also:* ADDED ENTRY; ENTRY

MANDATE The authority vested in an AGENCY, i.e., its mission. For example, the mandate of a provincial or state ARCHIVES (3) is the administration of the ARCHIVES under its jurisdiction. A mandate is fulfilled by means of FUNCTIONS.

MANIFEST A list or invoice of cargo or passengers, as of a ship or plane, usually containing marks or indications of contents or commodity, consignee, and other pertinent information for use at terminals or customhouses. (AAT)

MANUSCRIPT A handwritten or typed DOCUMENT. A typed DOCUMENT is more precisely called a TYPESCRIPT. *See also:* MANUSCRIPTS

Manuscript Box *See:* ARCHIVES BOX/CONTAINER

Manuscript Collection *See:* COLLECTION (1,2)

MANUSCRIPT CURATOR A person professionally educated, trained, experienced, and engaged in the following activities in a MANUSCRIPT REPOSITORY: solicitation, ACQUISITION, PROCESSING, PRESERVATION, REFERENCE SERVICE, and OUTREACH, including EXHIBITION and publication. In the United States, manuscript curators are also called ARCHIVISTS. *See also:* RECORDS MANAGER

MANUSCRIPT GROUP A term used to express the concept of RECORD GROUP when applied to RECORDS/ARCHIVES created by private persons or organizations. *See also:* COLLECTION (2)

MANUSCRIPT REPOSITORY An institution that collects PAPERS, MANUSCRIPTS, and, frequently, RECORDS/ARCHIVES of other institutions, usually in accordance with a predetermined ACQUISITION POLICY. *See also:* ARCHIVES (3)

MANUSCRIPTS DOCUMENTS of MANUSCRIPT character usually having historical or literary value or significance. The term is variously used to refer to ARCHIVES, to artificial COLLECTIONS of DOCUMENTS acquired from various sources usually according to a plan but without regard to PROVENANCE, and to individual DOCUMENTS acquired by a MANUSCRIPT REPOSITORY because of their significance. *See also:* PAPERS; RECORD

Manuscripts, Illuminated *See:* ILLUMINATED MANUSCRIPTS

MAP A DOCUMENT depicting in graphic or photogrammetric form, normally to scale and usually on a flat MEDIUM, a selection of material or abstract features on or in relation to the surface of the earth or of a heavenly body. (ICA) *See also:* PLAN

MARC AMC Format *See:* USMARC FORMAT FOR ARCHIVAL AND MANUSCRIPTS CONTROL (USMARC AMC)

MARC Format *See:* USMARC FORMAT

Marginal Note *See:* MARGINALIA

MARGINALIA Information recorded in the margin of a DOCUMENT. Marginalia is also referred to as marginal note(s). (ICA)

Marking *See:* STAMPING

Mass Deacidification *See:* DEACIDIFICATION

MASTER A COPY of a DOCUMENT or, in some processes, the original DOCUMENT, from which COPIES can be made. (ICA)

MASTER NEGATIVE A duplicate of the camera (original) NEGATIVE FILM used to generate REPRODUCTIONS.

MEDIUM The physical material in or on which information may be recorded (e.g., clay tablet, PAPYRUS, PAPER, PARCHMENT, FILM, MAGNETIC TAPE). *See also:* FORM (2)

MEMORANDUM 1. A DOCUMENT recording information used for internal communication and intended for future reference. (ICA)
2. A DOCUMENT drawn up in support of a case in court.

Memorandum Book *See:* COMMONPLACE BOOK

METADATA Data describing data and data systems; that is, the structure of databases, their characteristics, location, and usage.

METRIC SIZE An international measure for PAPER based on the subdivisions of a square meter. *See also:* LEGAL SIZE; LETTER SIZE

Microcard *See:* MICRO-OPAQUE

MICROCOPY A COPY, usually obtained by photography, in a size too small to be read without MAGNIFICATION. (ICA)

MICROFICHE A flexible transparent sheet of FILM bearing a number of MICROIMAGES arranged in horizontal rows and vertical columns, normally having an identifying strip legible without MAGNIFICATION. (ICA)

Microfiche Camera *See:* STEP-AND-REPEAT CAMERA

MICROFILM A fine grain, high resolution FILM used to record MICROIMAGES. The types of FILM commonly used are SILVER GELATIN FILM, VESICULAR FILM, and DIAZO FILM. *See also:* ROLL

Microfilm Camera *See:* PLANETARY CAMERA; ROTARY CAMERA; STEP-AND-REPEAT CAMERA

MICROFILM INSPECTION Periodic examination of stored microfilmed RECORDS to detect deterioration or damage (e.g., BRITTLENESS, buckling, mold or mildew, discoloration, or fading). *See also:* MICROFILM QUALITY CONTROL

MICROFILM JACKET A protective transparent holder into which individual strips of MICROFILM may be inserted.

Microfilm Processing *See:* PROCESSING (2)

MICROFILM QUALITY CONTROL Those procedures required to ensure that quality standards for MICROFILM are met. Procedures include, but are not limited to, such tests as those for residual thiosulfate, DENSITY, RESOLUTION, and base fog as defined by AIIM/ANSI standards. *See also:* ARCHIVAL QUALITY; MICROFILM INSPECTION

MICROFILM STRIP A segment of MICROFILM that is usually inserted into a MICROFILM JACKET.

Microfilm/Microfiche Reader *See:* READER (MICROFORM)

Microfilm/Microfiche Reader-Printer *See:* READER-PRINTER (MICROFORM)

Microfilm Target *See:* TARGET

MICROFORM A generic term for any MEDIUM, transparent or opaque, including, but not limited to, APERTURE CARDS, MICROFICHE, MICROFILM STRIPS, and ROLLS (2).

MICROFORM PUBLICATION The publication on MICROFORM, usually in ROLLS (2) or on MICROFICHE, of ORIGINAL DOCUMENTS with necessary TARGETS and explanatory materials.

Microform Reader *See:* READER (MICROFORM)

MICROGRAPHICS The technology and processes used to record information in MICROFORM.

MICROIMAGE An IMAGE too small to be read without MAGNIFICATION. (ICA)

MICRO-OPAQUE MICROIMAGES arranged in similar manner to those on a MICROFICHE but on an opaque MEDIUM. A MICRO-OPAQUE is also called a microcard or microprint.

Microphotography *See:* MICROGRAPHICS

Microprint *See:* MICRO-OPAQUE

Migrated Archives *See:* REMOVED ARCHIVES

MINUTES MEMORANDA or NOTES (2) of a PROCEEDING.

Mobile Shelving *See:* COMPACT SHELVING

Monetary Appraisal *See:* VALUATION

MORTGAGE A pledge or security of particular property for the payment of a debt or the performance of some other obligation.

MOTION PICTURE A sequence of IMAGES on roll FILM or VIDEOTAPE that as the FILM or tape is advanced, presents the illusion of motion or movement. Motion pictures are also called moving images and, in Canada, cinefilm.

Moving Images *See:* MOTION PICTURE

MULTILEVEL DESCRIPTION The preparation of DESCRIPTIONS (2) that are related to one another in a part-to-whole relationship and that need complete identification of both parts and the comprehensive whole in multiple DESCRIPTIVE RECORDS. (RAD) *See also:* HIERARCHICAL DESCRIPTIVE SYSTEM; LEVEL OF DESCRIPTION

MUSTER ROLL A list of troops actually present, made on the day of muster or review of troops in order to take account of their condition. Muster rolls are used as the paymaster's voucher for the pay issued. (AAT)

NARROWER TERM In a THESAURUS, a term which denotes a concept which is narrower than that of a term with a broader, more general meaning. For example, "Chairs" is narrower than "Furniture." (HARRODS) *See also:* BROADER TERM; RELATED TERM

Naturalness *See:* ARCHIVAL NATURE

NEAR-PRINT DOCUMENTS The product of any of the techniques of publishing or reproducing in quantity by a process other than ordinary printing. Examples of processes include, but are not limited to, hectograph, multilith, mimeograph, electrostatic, and thermographic. Near-print documents are also called processed documents.

NEGATIVE A photographic IMAGE with reversed POLARITY or, if colored, complementary tonal values to those of the original. (ICA)

NEGATIVE MICROFILM A MICROFILM consisting of NEGATIVE IMAGES. (ICA)

Nitrate film *See:* CELLULOSE NITRATE FILM

Non-Aqueous Deacidification *See:* DEACIDIFICATION

NONCURRENT RECORDS RECORDS no longer needed by their CREATOR to conduct current business. *See also:* CURRENT RECORDS; SEMICURRENT RECORDS

NONRECORD MATERIAL Documentary materials excluded from the legal definition of RECORDS in some political jurisdictions. For example, the United States Government defines nonrecord material to include material such as unofficial copies of DOCUMENTS kept only for convenience or reference, stocks of publications and NEAR-PRINT DOCUMENTS, and library or museum material intended solely for reference or EXHIBITION.

NONTEXTUAL RECORDS/ARCHIVES RECORDS/ARCHIVES of a pictorial, graphic, or aural form, as opposed to textual form. Nontextual records/archives include such DOCUMENTS as PHOTOGRAPHS, FILMS, illustrations, diagrams, PLANS, and SOUND RECORDINGS. *See also:* TEXTUAL RECORDS/ARCHIVES

NOTE 1. An informal statement in writing.

2. An ABSTRACT or a MEMORANDUM.

3. A unilateral INSTRUMENT containing an express and absolute promise of signer to pay to a

specified person, or order, or bearer, a definite sum of money at a specified time.

4. A written diplomatic or other official communication.

Numerical Arrangement *See:* ARRANGEMENT

OATH Any form of attestation by which persons signify that they are bound in conscience to perform an act faithfully and truthfully. (AAT)

OCR *See:* OPTICAL CHARACTER RECOGNITION (OCR)

Office File *See:* CONVENIENCE FILE

OFFICE OF ORIGIN The CORPORATE BODY or administrative unit in which a group of RECORDS are created or received and accumulated in the conduct of its business. *See also:* CONTROLLING AGENCY; CREATOR; TRANSFERRING AGENCY

OFFICE OF RECORD An office designated to maintain the RECORD COPIES of DOCUMENTS for an organization.

Official Copy *See:* RECORD COPY

OFFICIAL RECORD A RECORD created or received by, sanctioned by, or proceeding from an officer acting in an official capacity. In law, an official record has the legally recognized and judicially enforceable quality of establishing some fact.

OFF-LINE PROCESSING DATA PROCESSING performed independently of a central processing unit. *See also:* BATCH PROCESSING; ON-LINE PROCESSING

Off-Site Storage *See:* REMOTE STORAGE

ON-LINE PROCESSING DATA PROCESSING that is directly controlled by the central processing unit of a computer, usually in which individual RECORDS (2) or transactions are processed immediately by the central processing unit without batching. (ALA) *See also:* BATCH PROCESSING; OFF-LINE PROCESSING

OPEN ENTRY A single ENTRY (2) in a CATALOG or INDEX that represents a group of like pieces of information to which new, individual pieces can be added.

OPEN FILE 1. A FILE (1,2) to which DOCUMENTS are being added. (ICA)

2. A FILE (1,2) with no restrictions as to ACCESS, as distinct from a CLOSED FILE (2). (ICA)

OPEN INDEX An INDEX into which additional entries may be added.

OPEN REEL FILM/TAPE A general term used for tape or FILM supplied on its own REEL and not contained in a CARTRIDGE or CASSETTE. The tape or FILM is threaded, usually by hand, through the mechanism of its machine and is then wound on a separate take-up reel. *See also:* CARTRIDGE; CASSETTE

Operational Records *See:* PROGRAM RECORDS

Operational Value *See:* ADMINISTRATIVE VALUE

OPTICAL CHARACTER RECOGNITION (OCR) The detection, identification, and acceptance by a machine of printed characters using light-sensitive devices. (ALA) *See also:* SCANNER

OPTICAL DISC A device that allows the storage of either digital or analog signals on a disc. The data is retrieved through the use of a laser. An optical disc is also known as a laser disc. *See also:* COMPACT DISC; VIDEODISC

ORAL HISTORY The products of planned oral interviews with individuals, usually in the form of SOUND RECORDINGS or TRANSCRIPTS (3) thereof, intended for research use.

ORDINANCE A governmental, especially municipal, STATUTE or regulation.

Organicity *See:* ARCHIVAL NATURE

Orientation Interview *See:* REFERENCE INTERVIEW

ORIGINAL DOCUMENT The initially created DOCUMENT as distinguished from any COPY thereof. (ICA)

Original Order *See:* RESPECT FOR ORIGINAL ORDER (PRINCIPLE OF)

Original Record *See:* ORIGINAL DOCUMENT

Originating Agency/Office *See:* OFFICE OF ORIGIN

OUT-GUIDE A device, usually containing borrowing information, that physically replaces material that has been removed from its location.

OUTREACH PROGRAM Organized activities of ARCHIVES (3) or MANUSCRIPT REPOSITORIES intended to acquaint potential USERS with their HOLDINGS and their research and reference value. *See also:* USER EDUCATION

Packing Checklist *See:* CHECKLIST

PAGE One side of a LEAF. (ICA)

PAGINATION 1. The act of numbering PAGES in a DOCUMENT. (ICA)

2. The results of this action. (ICA) *See also:* FOLIATION

PALEOGRAPHY The study and interpretation of ancient and medieval script and DOCUMENTS. The term is now also used to refer to the study and interpretation of any script.

PALIMPSEST Writing material, usually PARCHMENT, that has been written upon more than once, often with remnants of earlier imperfectly erased writing still visible.

PAMPHLET BOX A container intended primarily for holding flimsy or unbound materials such as newspaper clippings or pamphlets.

PAPER A MEDIUM commonly made from pulped cellulose fibers (derived mainly from wood, rags, or certain grasses) suspended in water, formed into sheets on a screen, and dried.

PAPERS 1. Personal and family (and estate) DOCUMENTS/ARCHIVES as distinct from the DOCUMENTS/ARCHIVES of organizations called RECORDS.

2. A general term used to designate more than one type of MANUSCRIPT material. (ICA) *See also:* MANUSCRIPTS; PERSONAL PAPERS; PRIVATE RECORDS/ARCHIVES

Paperwork Management *See:* RECORDS MANAGEMENT

PAPYRUS 1. A MEDIUM made from a waterplant by the ancient Egyptians, Greeks, and Romans by soaking, pounding, and drying thin slices of its pith laid crosswise.

2. A DOCUMENT on PAPYRUS. (ICA)

PARCHMENT 1. Traditionally, the skin of an animal, usually a sheep or goat, prepared for use as a writing material. Today, this term is sometimes used interchangeably with VELLUM.

2. A DOCUMENT on PARCHMENT. (ICA) *See also:* VELLUM

Pass Slip *See:* TRANSFER SLIP

PATENT 1. A grant of some privilege, property, or authority, made by the government or sovereign of a country to one or more individuals.

2. A grant made by the government to an inventor, conveying and securing to the grantee the exclusive right to make, use, and sell his/her invention for a term of years.

Patrimonial Archives *See:* FAMILY (AND ESTATE) ARCHIVES

Pending File *See:* TICKLER FILE

Periodic Transfer *See:* TRANSFER

PERMANENCE The ability of a material to remain stable over time and resist chemical action either from internal impurities or the surrounding environment. *See also:* DURABILITY; PERMANENT/DURABLE PAPER

PERMANENT/DURABLE PAPER A PAPER made to resist the effects of aging. DURABILITY is reflected by the retention of physical qualities under continual use, while PERMANENCE is judged by resistance to chemical action either from impurities in the PAPER or from environmental conditions. Acid is the most important agent in the breakdown of the cellulose fiber chains and the resultant degeneration of the PAPER. While a PAPER with a pH value of 7 may be considered neutral or acid-free, an alkaline-buffered PAPER or ALKALINE RESERVE PAPER that has a pH value of 8.5 and a 3 to 5 percent alkaline reserve, is preferable for archival materials. Such buffered PAPERS not only are stable, but also resist ACID MIGRATION and contamination from the environment. (ALA) *See also:* DURABILITY; PERMANENCE; pH

Permanent Records *See:* ARCHIVES

Permanent Value *See:* ARCHIVAL VALUE

Permanent Withdrawal *See:* DEACCESSIONING

PERMIT A DOCUMENT which grants a person the right to do something not forbidden by law but not allowable without such authority. (AAT)

PERMUTED INDEX An INDEX created by rotating terms within a group of terms so that each term serves as an ACCESS POINT. *See also:* KEYWORD AND CONTEXT INDEX (KWAC); KEYWORD IN CONTEXT INDEX (KWIC); KEYWORD OUT OF CONTEXT INDEX (KWOC)

Personal File *See:* CONVENIENCE FILE

PERSONAL PAPERS The private DOCUMENTS accumulated by or belonging to an individual and subject to his/her DISPOSITION. *See also:* OFFICIAL RECORD; PAPERS

PERTINENCE (PRINCIPLE OF) A principle, now rejected, for the arrangement of ARCHIVES in terms of their subject CONTENT regardless of their PROVENANCE and original order. (ICA) *See also:* FUNCTIONAL PERTINENCE; TERRITORIAL PERTINENCE

PETITION A written request to an authority for the performance of a specific action. (ICA)

pH A measure of the acidity or alkalinity of PAPER. Also referred to as hydrogen ion concentration, pH is expressed in terms of a logarithmic scale from 0 to 14. Seven is the neutral point; values above 7 are alkaline; values below 7 are acid.

Acidity is a major cause of PAPER deterioration. *See also:* BUFFERING AGENT; PERMANENT/DURABLE PAPER

PHASED PRESERVATION An approach to PRESERVATION that emphasizes broad stabilizing actions to protect the entire HOLDINGS of a REPOSITORY, rather than the concentration of resources solely on ITEM level treatment. Such an approach includes, but is not limited to, preservation planning and surveys to establish priorities, disaster planning, controlling the storage environment, performing HOLDINGS MAINTENANCE, and selective treatment of materials. *See also:* ENVIRONMENTAL CONTROL; HOLDINGS MAINTENANCE; DISASTER PLAN

Phono Disc *See:* SOUND RECORDING

Phonograph Album/Record *See:* SOUND RECORDING

Phonotape *See:* AUDIOTAPE

PHOTOCOPY A COPY produced on or by means of sensitized material by the action of light or other radiant energy with or without intermediate NEGATIVE. (ICA)

PHOTOGRAPH An IMAGE produced on photosensitive material by EXPOSURE to light and subsequent chemical development. PHOTOGRAPHS are also called still pictures. *See also:* NEGATIVE; POSITIVE; PRINT

PHOTOGRAPHIC RECORDS/ARCHIVES RECORDS/ARCHIVES in the form of PHOTOGRAPHS, including NEGATIVES and PRINTS. *See also:* AUDIO-VISUAL RECORDS/ARCHIVES; ICONOGRAPHIC RECORDS/ARCHIVES

PHOTOSTAT (TM) 1. A trade name for photocopying cameras, chemicals, and sensitive materials that produce paper copies with the same POLARITY as the original.
2. A COPY produced by this process. (ICA)

PHYSICAL CONTROL A subset of ADMINISTRATIVE CONTROL that is established over the physical aspects (such as quantity or location) of DOCUMENTS in a RECORDS CENTER or ARCHIVES (2). *See also:* INTELLECTUAL CONTROL; PROCESS CONTROL

Physical Custody *See:* CUSTODY

Physical Form *See:* FORM (2)

PHYSICAL RECORD In DATA PROCESSING, a RECORD (2) defined in terms of its form or the physical space it requires. *See also:* LOGICAL RECORD

Piece *See:* ITEM

Placard *See:* POSTER

PLAN A DOCUMENT in graphic or photogrammetric form depicting the arrangement in horizontal section of a structure, piece of ground, etc. (ICA) *See also:* MAP

PLANETARY CAMERA A microfilm camera so constructed that the ORIGINAL DOCUMENT and FILM are stationary and in parallel planes during EXPOSURE. The DOCUMENT is changed and the FILM advanced after EXPOSURE. A PLANETARY CAMERA is also called a flatbed camera. *See also:* ROTARY CAMERA; STEP-AND-REPEAT CAMERA

POLARITY A term used to indicate the change (reversal) in or retention of the dark to light relationship of an IMAGE or COPY as compared with the original. (ICA)

Policy, Access *See:* ACCESS POLICY

Policy, Acquisition *See:* ACQUISITION POLICY

PORTFOLIO 1. A flat, portable case for the storage of large or fragile DOCUMENTS. (ICA)
2. The position and duties of an officer; his/her COMPETENCE.

POSITIVE A photographic IMAGE having the same POLARITY as the original. (ICA)

POSITIVE MICROFILM MICROFILM consisting of IMAGES having the same POLARITY as the original.

POST-COORDINATE INDEXING SYSTEM An indexing system whereby DOCUMENTS are initially indexed by all applicable individual terms. In RETRIEVAL (2), the user combines separate terms to form the complex concepts desired. *See also:* PRE-COORDINATE INDEXING SYSTEM

POSTER A DOCUMENT, usually printed on one side of a single SHEET of PAPER and often illustrated, posted to advertise or publicize something. A POSTER is also called a placard. (ICA)

POSTING UP The practice of indexing a DOCUMENT not only by the terms precisely describing its subject, but also by one or more BROADER TERMS. (ARMA)

PRECISION RATIO A measure of the ability of an INFORMATION RETRIEVAL SYSTEM to suppress irrelevant DOCUMENTS in searching. Precision is defined as the ratio of the relevant DOCUMENTS retrieved to the total number of DOCUMENTS retrieved. *See also:* RECALL RATIO

PRE-COORDINATE INDEXING SYSTEM An indexing system by which terms are combined at the time of indexing a DOCUMENT. Thus, the indexer, not the searcher, identifies terms or phrases that combine to form complex concepts. *See also:* POST-COORDINATE INDEXING SYSTEM

Preliminary Inventory *See:* INVENTORY

Preliminary Survey *See:* RECORDS SURVEY

PRESERVATION The totality of processes and operations involved in the stabilization and protection of DOCUMENTS against damage or deterioration and in the treatment of damaged or deteriorated

DOCUMENTS. PRESERVATION may also include the transfer of information to another MEDIUM, such as MICROFILM. *See also:* CONSERVATION; PHASED PRESERVATION

Preservation Laboratory *See:* CONSERVATION LABORATORY

PRESERVATION MICROFILMING The creation of archivally acceptable MICROFILM to preserve the informational CONTENT of DOCUMENTS that either are in poor condition or that were created utilizing poor quality materials, as well as to preserve originals from deterioration through repeated handling and use. *See also:* ACQUISITION MICROFILM; DISPOSAL MICROFILMING; SECURITY MICROFILMING

Preservation, Phased *See:* PHASED PRESERVATION

PRESERVATION PHOTOCOPYING The use of photocopies to preserve the informational CONTENT of DOCUMENTS that either are in poor condition or that were created utilizing poor quality materials, as well as to preserve originals from deterioration through repeated handling and use. Such photocopies are made on PERMANENT/DURABLE PAPER using an archivally acceptable photocopying process.

Press Copy *See:* LETTERPRESS COPYBOOK

PRIMARY VALUE The value that RECORDS/ARCHIVES possess, by virtue of their CONTENTS, for the continued transaction of the business that gave rise to their creation. *See also:* SECONDARY VALUE

Princeton File *See:* PAMPHLET BOX

Principal Copy *See:* RECORD COPY

PRINT 1. A COPY of a photographic IMAGE made on a light sensitive surface.
2. A picture or design reproduced by any printing process, including both proofs and final versions.

PRINTED ARCHIVES The published (including printed and NEAR-PRINT) DOCUMENTS of an organization that have ARCHIVAL VALUE.

PRIVACY The right of an individual to be secure from unauthorized disclosure of information about oneself that is contained in DOCUMENTS/ARCHIVES.

Private Papers *See:* PERSONAL PAPERS

PRIVATE RECORDS/ARCHIVES RECORDS/ARCHIVES of nongovernmental PROVENANCE. *See also:* PUBLIC RECORDS

Privileged Information/Records *See:* RESTRICTED INFORMATION/RECORDS

PROCEEDINGS A RECORD of business transacted at a meeting or conference. PROCEEDINGS are also called transactions.

PROCESS CONTROL A subset of ADMINISTRATIVE CONTROL established over actions performed on DOCUMENTS in a RECORDS CENTER or ARCHIVES (2). This information includes past, current, and planned actions on the RECORDS as opposed to information contained therein. *See also:* INTELLECTUAL CONTROL; PHYSICAL CONTROL

Processed Document *See:* NEAR-PRINT DOCUMENTS

PROCESSING 1. The activities of accessioning, arranging, describing, and properly storing archival materials.
2. The treatment of exposed photographic material to make the latent IMAGE(S) visible. (ICA)

Processing, Data *See:* DATA PROCESSING

PRODUCTION PAPERS MANUSCRIPTS and various kinds and stages of proofs (printer's galleys, etc.) produced in the process of printing and publishing books and literary works. *See also:* LITERARY MANUSCRIPTS

PROGRAM RECORDS RECORDS relating to the substantive FUNCTIONS of an organization, i.e., the program for which it is responsible, as distinct from ADMINISTRATIVE RECORDS. In Canada, program records are known as operational records.

Project File *See:* CASE FILE

PROPOSAL An offer, by one person to another, of terms and conditions with reference to some work or undertaking, or for the transfer of property, the acceptance whereof will make a CONTRACT between them. (BLACKS)

PROVENANCE 1. The organization or individual that created, accumulated, and/or maintained and used RECORDS in the conduct of business prior to their TRANSFER to a RECORDS CENTER, ARCHIVES (2), or MANUSCRIPT REPOSITORY. *See also:* FUNCTIONAL PROVENANCE; PROVENANCE (PRINCIPLE OF); RESPECT FOR ORIGINAL ORDER (PRINCIPLE OF)
2. Information regarding the origin and CUSTODIAL HISTORY of DOCUMENTS.

PROVENANCE (PRINCIPLE OF) The principle that RECORDS/ARCHIVES of the same PROVENANCE must not be intermingled with those of any other PROVENANCE; frequently referred to as "respect des fonds." *See also:* ARCHIVAL INTEGRITY; RESPECT FOR ORIGINAL ORDER (PRINCIPLE OF)

PROVENANCE ACCESS The use of PROVENANCE information to provide ACCESS to ARCHIVES. This technique is based on the understanding that certain organizations, AGENCIES, and individuals performed certain FUNCTIONS, or carried out certain activities, and therefore accumulated RECORDS containing certain types of information.

Provenance access is a complementary retrieval method to SUBJECT ACCESS.

Public Programming *See:* OUTREACH PROGRAM

PUBLIC RECORDS 1. DOCUMENTS created or received and accumulated by government AGENCIES in the conduct of public business, which may or may not be open to public inspection. *See also:* PRIVATE RECORDS/ARCHIVES
2. DOCUMENTS open to public inspection.

Pulping *See:* MACERATION

PULPIT LADDER A safety ladder having an extended top shelf, used for retrieving RECORDS stored on high shelves. (ARMA)

PUNCHED CARD/TAPE A PAPER card or tape on which data are recorded by punching holes in specified positions in accordance with a predesignated, usually machine-readable, code.

Purging *See:* WEEDING

Quality Control (Microfilm) *See:* MICROFILM QUALITY CONTROL

Quartz Lamp *See:* ULTRAVIOLET LAMP

QUESTIONED DOCUMENT A DOCUMENT whose origin or authorship has been challenged and whose authenticity is in doubt. *See also:* FORGERY

Random Access *See:* DIRECT ACCESS

Range *See:* ROW

Reader *See:* RESEARCHER

READER (MICROFORM) An optical device for viewing a projected and enlarged MICROIMAGE. (ICA) *See also:* READER-PRINTER (MICROFORM)

Reader Service *See:* REFERENCE SERVICE

READER-PRINTER (MICROFORM) A READER (MICROFORM) with the added capability of reproducing an enlarged MICROIMAGE in HARD COPY. *See also:* READER (MICROFORM)

Reading File *See:* CHRONOLOGICAL FILE

Reading Room *See:* RESEARCH ROOM

REAPPRAISAL The process of reevaluating the HOLDINGS of an ARCHIVES (3) or MANUSCRIPT REPOSITORY to determine which HOLDINGS should be retained and which should be deaccessioned. REAPPRAISAL is also known as retention review. *See also:* DEACCESSIONING

RECALL RATIO A measure of the ability of an INFORMATION RETRIEVAL SYSTEM to retrieve relevant information. Recall is expressed as the proportion of relevant DOCUMENTS known to be in a system that are retrieved in a given search or set of searches. *See also:* PRECISION RATIO

RECORD 1. A DOCUMENT created or received and maintained by an AGENCY, organization, or individual in pursuance of legal obligations or in the transaction of business. *See also:* DOCUMENT; ITEM; OFFICIAL RECORD
2. In DATA PROCESSING, a grouping of interrelated data elements forming the basic unit of a FILE (3).

RECORD COPY That COPY of a DOCUMENT that is placed on file as the official copy. A record copy is also referred to as the file copy.

RECORD GROUP A body of organizationally related RECORDS established on the basis of PROVENANCE by an ARCHIVES (3) for control purposes. A RECORD GROUP constitutes the ARCHIVES (or the part thereof in the CUSTODY of an archival institution) of an autonomous recordkeeping CORPORATE BODY. COLLECTIVE RECORD GROUPS and GENERAL RECORD GROUPS represent modifications of this basic concept for convenience in ARRANGEMENT, DESCRIPTION, and REFERENCE SERVICE. *See also:* COLLECTION; FONDS; MANUSCRIPT GROUP; SUBGROUP

Record Group, Collective *See:* COLLECTIVE RECORD GROUP

Record Group, General *See:* GENERAL RECORD GROUP

Record Series *See:* SERIES

Record Subgroup *See:* SUBGROUP

RECORD TYPE The functional title for a RECORD or SERIES, such as LICENSE, proclamation, or REGISTER. The title normally specifies or at least implies function or use, and often implies the basic layout of information. *See also:* FORM (2); GENRE

Records Administration *See:* RECORDS MANAGEMENT

Records Administrator *See:* RECORDS MANAGER

RECORDS ANALYST A specialist in the examination and evaluation of systems and procedures related to the creation, processing, storing, and DISPOSITION of RECORDS. *See also:* RECORDS MANAGER; RECORDS OFFICER

RECORDS CENTER A facility for the low-cost storage, maintenance, and reference use of SEMICURRENT RECORDS pending their ultimate DISPOSITION. Records centers are also referred to as intermediate storage or limbo.

RECORDS CENTER CARTON/CONTAINER A corrugated cardboard box designed to hold approximately one cubic foot of RECORDS, either legal or letter size, and used chiefly in RECORDS CENTERS. *See also:* ARCHIVES BOX/CONTAINER

Records Control Schedule *See:* RECORDS SCHEDULE

Records Creator *See:* CREATOR

Records Disposal *See:* DISPOSITION

Records Disposal Schedule *See:* RECORDS SCHEDULE

Records Disposition *See:* DISPOSITION

Records Inventory *See:* INVENTORY

Records Liaison Officer *See:* RECORDS OFFICER

RECORDS MANAGEMENT A field of management responsible for the systematic control of the creation, maintenance, use, and DISPOSITION of RECORDS.

Records Management Officer *See:* RECORDS OFFICER

RECORDS MANAGER An individual within an organization who is responsible for managing the LIFE CYCLE of RECORDS created and received by the organization. A records manager is sometimes called a records administrator. *See also:* ARCHIVIST; MANUSCRIPT CURATOR; RECORDS OFFICER

RECORDS OFFICER An administrative unit's representative to a central records management/archival program for an entire organization, government, etc. The records officer conducts the unit's RECORDS MANAGEMENT program in conjunction with and/or under the oversight of the central program. A records officer is also called a records liaison officer. *See also:* RECORDS MANAGER

Records Retention Plan *See:* RECORDS SCHEDULE

Records Retention Schedule *See:* RECORDS SCHEDULE

Records Retirement *See:* DISPOSITION

RECORDS SCHEDULE A DOCUMENT describing RECORDS of an AGENCY, organization, or administrative unit, establishing a timetable for their LIFE CYCLE, and providing authorization for their DISPOSITION. A records schedule is also referred to as a comprehensive records schedule, disposal schedule, records retention schedule, records disposition schedule, retention schedule, and transfer schedule. *See also:* GENERAL RECORDS SCHEDULE

RECORDS SURVEY A SURVEY that gathers basic information on the RECORDS of an organization with respect to their quantity, FORM (2), location, physical condition, storage facilities, rate of accumulation, and uses for the purpose of planning RECORDS MANAGEMENT and/or archival operations and activities.

Records Transfer *See:* TRANSFER

Records, Unscheduled *See:* UNSCHEDULED RECORDS

RECTO A right-hand PAGE of a book or the front of a separate SHEET. *See also:* VERSO

REDUCTION RATIO A measure of the number of times a given linear dimension of a DOCUMENT is reduced when photographed, expressed as 12X, 14X, 16X. (ICA)

REEL A MICROFILM, MOTION PICTURE, FILM, or MAGNETIC TAPE roll carrier consisting of a circular core and two circular flanges. (ICA) *See also:* ROLL (2)

Reel to Reel Film/Tape *See:* OPEN REEL FILM/TAPE

Reference *See:* REFERENCE SERVICE

Reference Analysis *See:* USE/USER STUDY

REFERENCE COPY A COPY of a RECORD used primarily for consultation purposes.

REFERENCE INTERVIEW The formal conversation that an ARCHIVIST conducts with each RESEARCHER. Reference interviews are conducted to ascertain the identity of the RESEARCHER; to determine his/her information needs and purposes of research; to guide the RESEARCHER to appropriate access tools and relevant sources; to inform him/her of basic procedures and limitations on ACCESS, handling of DOCUMENTS, and REPRODUCTION; and to evaluate the success of the research visit and the effectiveness of the REFERENCE SERVICE offered to the RESEARCHER. The initial reference interview is often referred to as an orientation interview; the interview at the end of a research visit is often referred to as an exit interview. *See also:* FOLLOW-UP INTERVIEW

REFERENCE NUMBER The unique number assigned to SERIES, file units, and/or ITEMS to facilitate storage and RETRIEVAL.

Reference Request *See:* REQUEST

Reference Room *See:* RESEARCH ROOM

REFERENCE SERVICE The range of activities involved in assisting RESEARCHERS using archival materials.

Reference/Research Value *See:* INFORMATIONAL VALUE

REFILE The return of a file unit or DOCUMENT to its storage location after use. *See also:* INTERFILE

REGISTER   1. A list, often in the form of a VOLUME, of items, names, events, actions, etc. The ENTRIES (2) are usually in numerical or chronological sequence. Registers often accomplish the legal function of providing evidence of facts and acts and may also serve as a FINDING AID to RECORDS, such as a register of LETTERS sent.
2. The FINDING AID developed in the Manuscript Division of the Library of Congress to describe groups of PAPERS and RECORDS by giving their PROVENANCE and conditions of ACCESS and use; scope and general CONTENT, including INCLUSIVE DATES and BULK DATES; a biographical note about the person, family group, or organization whose material it is; its arrangement; a FOLDER LIST; and on occasion, selective INDEXES. *See also:* INVENTORY

REGISTRY   A unit of an AGENCY responsible for the creation, control, and maintenance of CURRENT RECORDS and/or SEMICURRENT RECORDS. A registry may exist at various organizational levels, such as central or departmental.

Registry Principle   *See:* RESPECT FOR ORIGINAL ORDER (PRINCIPLE OF)

REGISTRY SYSTEM   A system controlling the creation, maintenance, and use of CURRENT RECORDS and/or SEMICURRENT RECORDS through the use of formal REGISTERS, lists, and INDEXES. *See also:* REGISTRY

RELATED TERM   A notation under an ENTRY (2) in a THESAURUS or other AUTHORITY FILE that indicates other terms that are equal in specificity and should be considered for indexing or information retrieval. *See also:* BROADER TERM; NARROWER TERM

RELOCATION SITE   The emergency operating location from which an organization functions during an emergency.

REMOTE STORAGE   Off-site storage of RECORDS. (ARMA) *See also:* DISPERSAL

REMOVED ARCHIVES   ARCHIVES that have been removed from the country in which they were originally accumulated. Removed archives are sometimes called migrated, fugitive, or captured archives. *See also:* ALIENATION (2); ESTRAY; REPLEVIN

REPLEVIN   A legal action for the recovery of RECORDS/ARCHIVES by an AGENCY, organization, or individual claiming ownership of them.

REPORT   A DOCUMENT containing a presentation of facts or the record of some proceeding, investigation, or event. (ICA)

REPORTS MANAGEMENT   The application of RECORDS MANAGEMENT techniques to reporting practices. Reports management involves the establishment of a system for the creation, maintenance, and use of REPORTS.

REPOSITORY   A place where DOCUMENTS are kept. Repository is frequently used synonymously with depository. *See also:* ARCHIVES (2); MANUSCRIPT REPOSITORY

REPRODUCTION   An exact COPY of a DOCUMENT in CONTENT and FORM (2) but not necessarily in size and appearance. (ICA) *See also:* FACSIMILE

REPROGRAPHICS/REPROGRAPHY   All copying processes, including MICROGRAPHICS, using any form of radiant energy and all duplication and office printing processes including operations connected with such processes. (ICA)

REQUEST   A separate instance of in-person, mail, or telephone inquiry for information about or from the HOLDINGS of a RECORDS CENTER, ARCHIVES (2), or MANUSCRIPT REPOSITORY. A single request may result in more than one RETRIEVAL.

Required Field   *See:* FIELD

Research Request   *See:* REQUEST

RESEARCH ROOM   A room or area in a RECORDS CENTER, ARCHIVES (2), or MANUSCRIPT REPOSITORY where DOCUMENTS are consulted by RESEARCHERS under the supervision of and with the assistance of REPOSITORY personnel. A research room is also called a reading room or search room.

Research Tool   *See:* FINDING AID

RESEARCHER   An individual who consults DOCUMENTS, either by a visit to a RESEARCH ROOM or through mail or telephone contact, for information about or from the HOLDINGS of a RECORDS CENTER, ARCHIVES (2), or MANUSCRIPT REPOSITORY. A researcher is also called a reader or searcher. *See also:* USER

RESOLUTION   1. A measure of sharpness or detail in an IMAGE expressed as the number of lines per millimeter discernible in a standard test pattern IMAGE.
2. A formal expression of the opinion or will of an official body or a public assembly adopted by vote.

Respect des Fonds   *See:* PROVENANCE (PRINCIPLE OF)

RESPECT FOR ORIGINAL ORDER (PRINCIPLE OF)   The principle that ARCHIVES of a single PROVENANCE should retain the arrangement (including the REFERENCE NUMBERS) established by the CREATOR in order to preserve existing relationships and evidential significance and the usefulness of FINDING AIDS of the CREATOR. *See also:*

PROVENANCE (PRINCIPLE OF); RESTORATION OF ORIGINAL ORDER

Restoration Laboratory *See:* CONSERVATION LABORATORY

RESTORATION OF ORIGINAL ORDER The re-establishment of the original order of a group of accessioned DOCUMENTS whose order has been disturbed by accidental causes or through deliberate rearrangement conducted by persons or organizations that had CUSTODY of the material in its noncurrent life. *See also:* ARRANGEMENT; RESPECT FOR ORIGINAL ORDER (PRINCIPLE OF)

RESTRICTED ACCESS A limitation on the use of a body of DOCUMENTS or of single ITEMS containing information of a specific kind or in a particular form. The restriction may limit the use for a time to particular persons or classes of persons or may exclude all potential USERS. Restrictions may be imposed by law, by ARCHIVES (3) or MANUSCRIPT REPOSITORIES having CUSTODY of the material, or by officials of CONTROLLING AGENCIES or DONORS, and are enforced by the ARCHIVES (3) or MANUSCRIPT REPOSITORY. *See also:* ACCESS; CLEARANCE; SCREENING; SECURITY CLASSIFICATION

RESTRICTED INFORMATION/RECORDS Information or RECORDS to which ACCESS is limited. *See also:* CLOSED FILE (2); RESTRICTED ACCESS; SECURITY CLASSIFICATION

Restrictions *See:* RESTRICTED ACCESS

Retention and Disposition Plan *See:* RECORDS SCHEDULE

RETENTION PERIOD The length of time, usually based upon an estimate of the frequency of use for current and anticipated business, that RECORDS should be retained in offices or RECORDS CENTERS before they are transferred to an ARCHIVES (2) or otherwise disposed of.

Retention Plan/Schedule *See:* RECORDS SCHEDULE

Retention Review *See:* REAPPRAISAL

Retention Schedule *See:* RECORDS SCHEDULE

Retention Standard *See:* RETENTION PERIOD

Retirement *See:* DISPOSITION

RETRIEVAL 1. The process of locating and withdrawing a DOCUMENT or file unit from storage.
2. The action of recovering information on a given matter from stored data. (UN)

Reverse Chronological File *See:* CHRONOLOGICAL FILE

REVERSIBILITY (PRINCIPLE OF) The principle that no procedure or treatment should be undertaken on archival materials that cannot be undone if necessary.

ROLL 1. A rolled PAPER or PARCHMENT DOCUMENT or sequence of DOCUMENTS that have been attached end to end, usually for convenience of storage.
2. A length of MICROFILM on a carrier REEL.

ROTARY CAMERA A microfilm camera so constructed that the ORIGINAL DOCUMENT and FILM are moved simultaneously by connected transport mechanisms avoiding relative movement between FILM and DOCUMENT during EXPOSURE. (ICA) *See also:* PLANETARY CAMERA; STEP-AND-REPEAT CAMERA

ROW Two or more BAYS of shelving connected end to end along the same axis. A row is also called a run or range.

Run *See:* ROW

SAFETY FILM A FILM for photographic NEGATIVES and MOTION PICTURES that, unlike CELLULOSE NITRATE FILM, has a relatively non-flammable base. (Safety film gradually replaced nitrate FILM beginning in the 1930s.) Examples of safety film include cellulose diacetate, cellulose triacetate, and polyester. *See also:* CELLULOSE NITRATE FILM

SAMPLING In APPRAISAL, the selection of file units or ITEMS from a body of RECORDS made in such a way that, taken together, the ITEMS selected are representative of the whole.

SCANNER A device which converts an IMAGE of a DOCUMENT to electronic form for processing and storage. *See also:* OPTICAL CHARACTER RECOGNITION (OCR)

Schedule *See:* RECORDS SCHEDULE

Scheduled Records *See:* SCHEDULING

SCHEDULING The process of determining and recording in a RECORDS SCHEDULE the appropriate RETENTION PERIOD and ultimate DISPOSITION of SERIES. The RECORDS thus provided for are called scheduled records. *See also:* INVENTORY (2)

SCOPE AND CONTENT NOTE In DESCRIPTION, a narrative statement summarizing information on the characteristics of the described materials, including function and use as well as the kinds and types of information contained therein.

SCOPE NOTE A NOTE (2) that explains how a term in an AUTHORITY FILE or CLASSIFICATION PLAN/SCHEME is used.

SCREENING The examination of HOLDINGS to determine the presence of DOCUMENTS or information subject to RESTRICTED ACCESS. Screening is usually followed by SEGREGATION. *See also:* WEEDING

SEAL 1. A die or signet having a raised or incised emblem used to stamp an impression upon a receptive substance such as wax or lead.
2. A piece of wax, lead, or other material upon which such an impression has been made and attached to a DOCUMENT or applied to the face thereof. Originally serving as a means of AUTHENTICATION, seals have also been used to close DOCUMENTS. *See also:* COUNTERSEAL

Search Room *See:* RESEARCH ROOM

SEARCH STATEMENT In information retrieval, an individual search consisting of one search term or several linked terms formed to answer a particular inquiry.

Searcher *See:* RESEARCHER

SECONDARY VALUE The capacity of DOCUMENTS to serve as evidence or sources of information for persons and organizations other than their CREATOR. *See also:* PRIMARY VALUE

Section *See:* BAY

SECURITY An archival and RECORDS MANAGEMENT function concerned with the protection of DOCUMENTS from unauthorized ACCESS and/or damage or loss from fire, water, theft, mutilation, or unauthorized alteration or DESTRUCTION.

SECURITY CLASSIFICATION The restriction on ACCESS to and use of RECORDS/ARCHIVES or information therein imposed by a government in the interests of national security. The RECORDS or information concerned are referred to as classified records or classified information. (ICA) *See also:* DECLASSIFICATION; DOWNGRADE; RESTRICTED ACCESS

SECURITY COPY A COPY of a DOCUMENT made in order to preserve the information it contains in case the original is lost, damaged, or destroyed. *See also:* DISPERSAL; SECURITY MICROFILMING; VITAL RECORDS MANAGEMENT

SECURITY MICROFILMING The creation of MICROFILM to safeguard the information in DOCUMENTS. *See also:* ACQUISITION MICROFILM; DISPOSAL MICROFILMING; PRESERVATION MICROFILMING; SECURITY COPY; VITAL RECORDS MANAGEMENT

"SEE ALSO" REFERENCE A CROSS REFERENCE from a name, term, or phrase used as a HEADING (2) to one or more related names, terms, or phrases that are also used as HEADINGS (2). *See also:* "SEE" REFERENCE

"SEE" REFERENCE A CROSS REFERENCE to a name, term, or phrase used as a HEADING (2) from another form of the name, term, or phrase that is not used as a HEADING (2). *See also:* "SEE ALSO" REFERENCE

SEGREGATION The removal of restricted DOCUMENTS or information from FILES prior to making them available for use. *See also:* SCREENING

Selection *See:* APPRAISAL

Semi-Active Records *See:* SEMICURRENT RECORDS

SEMICURRENT RECORDS RECORDS required so infrequently in the conduct of current business that they should be moved to a HOLDING AREA or directly to a RECORDS CENTER, pending their ultimate DISPOSITION. *See also:* CURRENT RECORDS; NONCURRENT RECORDS

SEPARATION SHEET A FORM used to DOCUMENT the removal of one or more ITEMS from its/their original storage place. The separation sheet is filed in place of the removed ITEM(S). *See also:* CHARGE OUT; OUT-GUIDE

SERIES File units or DOCUMENTS arranged in accordance with a filing system or maintained as a unit because they result from the same accumulation or filing process, the same function, or the same activity; have a particular FORM (2); or because of some other relationship arising out of their creation, receipt, or use. A series is also known as a record series.

SERIES DESCRIPTION A written analysis describing a SERIES, usually including such elements as the series title, SCOPE AND CONTENT NOTE, size or VOLUME (2), INCLUSIVE DATES and/or BULK DATES of the material, arrangement, and subjects dealt with by the SERIES.

SERIES DESCRIPTIVE SYSTEM A system of DESCRIPTION in which the primary level of control is the SERIES rather than the FONDS or RECORD GROUP. The purpose of this system is to maintain control of SERIES over time. This system was first widely adopted in Australia in response to frequent administrative changes and the consequent existence of multi-provenance SERIES. *See also:* HIERARCHICAL DESCRIPTIVE SYSTEM

SHEET 1. A rectangular piece of PAPER, usually cut to a standard size.
2. A large piece of such PAPER with a number of PAGES printed on it, to be folded into a SIGNATURE (2) for binding.
3. An individual MAP or DRAWING, normally one of a SERIES.

SHELF A thin, flat length of metal, wood, or other material, usually one of a set, built into a frame, or between two uprights or standards which support it, for the storage of boxes or DOCUMENTS. (ICA)

SHELF LIST   A list of the HOLDINGS in a RECORDS CENTER, ARCHIVES (2), or MANUSCRIPT REPOSITORY arranged in the order of the contents of each SHELF. *See also:* LOCATION INDEX/REGISTER

Showcase *See:* DISPLAY CASE

SHREDDING   The DESTRUCTION of DOCUMENTS by mechanical cutting. (ICA)

SIGNATURE 1. The name or special mark of a person written on a DOCUMENT. The signature may be handwritten by the person in his/her own hand (AUTOGRAPH) or typed, or may be affixed by an office authorized to do so (as in posted proclamations or telegrams).

2. A large SHEET (2) that, when folded to PAGE size, forms one gathering or section of a VOLUME.

SILKING   A process formerly used in repair of a DOCUMENT by pasting silk gauze to the back or to both sides of a DOCUMENT. The process has been abandoned since its useful life is too short to be used for archival materials. *See also:* LAMINATION

SILVER GELATIN FILM A type of photographic FILM using light-sensitive silver halide particles, suspended in EMULSION, for the production of latent IMAGES that are stabilized by development, fixing, washing, and drying. Silver gelatin film, also referred to as silver halide film, when correctly manufactured, exposed, processed, and stored, is considered an archival MEDIUM.

Silver Halide Film *See:* SILVER GELATIN FILM

Simple Entry *See:* DIRECT ENTRY

SIZING 1. The application to the surface of PAPER, or incorporation during the formation of PAPER, of a substance designed to resist penetration by ink and improve printability.

2. The substance used for this purpose.

SKIPPET A small box, usually of wood or metal, used to protect a SEAL (2) attached to a DOCUMENT.

SLIDE   A single POSITIVE photographic IMAGE on transparent material held in a mount and intended for projection. *See also:* TRANSPARENCY

Solvent Lamination *See:* LAMINATION

SOUND RECORDING A disc, tape, filament, or other MEDIUM on which sound has been recorded. (ICA)

Sound Tape *See:* AUDIOTAPE

SOUNDEX (TM)   An alpha-numerical FILING SYSTEM that brings together all surnames that sound alike but may be spelled differently.

SOURCE DOCUMENT 1. In reprography, the ORIGINAL DOCUMENT from which copies are produced, normally containing text or other graphic matter that can be read or viewed without MAGNIFICATION. (ALA)

2. In DATA PROCESSING, an ORIGINAL DOCUMENT used to generate or prepare input into a DATA PROCESSING system. (ALA)

Space-saving Microfilming *See:* DISPOSAL MICROFILMING

Span Dates *See:* INCLUSIVE DATES

SPECIAL LIST A FINDING AID listing SERIES, file units, or DOCUMENTS to call attention to these particular items within a RECORD GROUP, to bring together information on all such items in several RECORD GROUPS relating to a particular topic, or to expand the descriptive detail provided in ENTRIES (3) in INVENTORIES. (SAA)

SPECIFICITY (OF INDEXING)   The required or agreed upon depth of indexing. *See also:* DEPTH INDEXING

SPLICING The joining together of two segments of roll FILM or tape.

STABILITY The ability of materials to resist decomposition. *See also:* PERMANENCE

STACK/STORAGE PLAN A plan of a stack or storage area indicating placement of shelving or other storage equipment and actual or intended use of the available space.

STACKS 1. The storage areas in a RECORDS CENTER, ARCHIVES (2), or MANUSCRIPT REPOSITORY for shelved material.

2. The shelving units in such a storage area.

Staging Area *See:* HOLDING AREA

STAMP 1. An impression made by public authority upon PAPER or PARCHMENT, and required by law to be used for certain legal PROCEEDINGS, conveyances, or CONTRACTS are required to be written, and for which a tax or duty is exacted.

2. A small label or strip of PAPER, bearing a particular device, printed and sold by a government, and required to be attached to mail matter, or to other articles subject to duty or excise.

3. An impression made upon a DOCUMENT denoting that it is the property of or in the legal CUSTODY of an ARCHIVES (3) or MANUSCRIPT REPOSITORY.

STAMPING   The placing of an identifying STAMP upon a DOCUMENT or the leaves thereof denoting that it is the property of or in the legal CUSTODY of an ARCHIVES (3) or MANUSCRIPT REPOSITORY. A REFERENCE NUMBER may also be placed within an identifying STAMP (3). Stamping is also called marking. *See also:* NUMBERING

STANDARDIZED FILING PLAN/SYSTEM A FILING PLAN/SYSTEM prescribed for all organizations of a particular type, or for all units of a particular organization, or for certain types of RECORDS common to several organizations.

STATUTE 1. An ACT of the legislature declaring, commanding, or prohibiting something. (BLACKS) 2. The written will of the legislature, solemnly expressed according to the forms necessary to constitute it the law of the state. (BLACKS)

STEP-AND-REPEAT CAMERA A microfilm camera that produces a series of separate IMAGES according to a predetermined sequence, usually in orderly rows and columns on 105mm MICROFILM, which is cut after PROCESSING (2) to create MICRO-FICHE. *See also:* PLANETARY CAMERA; ROTARY CAMERA

STEREOGRAPHICS Pairs of PHOTOGRAPHS taken from different angles that, when viewed through a stereoscope, are seen as a single picture apparently possessing depth or three dimensions.

Still Picture *See:* PHOTOGRAPH

STOP LIST A list of words, terms, or roots of words or terms to be ignored in indexing or information retrieval. *See also:* GO LIST

Stop Word List *See:* STOP LIST

Stripping *See:* WEEDING

Structural Guide *See:* GUIDE

SUBGROUP A body of related RECORDS within a RECORD GROUP or FONDS, corresponding to administrative subdivisions in the originating AGENCY or organization or, when that is not possible, to geographical, chronological, functional, or similar groupings of the material itself. When the creating body has a complex hierarchical structure, each SUBGROUP has as many subordinate SUBGROUPS as are necessary to reflect the levels of the hierarchical structure of the primary subordinate administrative unit. *See also:* RECORD GROUP

SUBHEADING A secondary HEADING (2) used as the division of a subject to delineate a particular group under the main HEADING (2).

SUBJECT ACCESS The use of information about the subject CONTENT of archival materials as ACCESS POINTS for their retrieval. Subject access is a complementary retrieval method to PROVE-NANCE ACCESS.

Subject Classification System *See:* CLASSIFICATION PLAN/SCHEME

Subject Entry *See:* ENTRY

SUBJECT FILE A FILE (1,2) in which the DOCUMENTS relate to a specific subject matter, frequently based upon a FILING PLAN/SYSTEM. Subject files are also called topical files. *See also:* CASE FILE

Subject Guide *See:* GUIDE (2)

SUBSERIES A body of DOCUMENTS within a SERIES readily identifiable in terms of filing arrangement, type, FORM (2), or CONTENT.

Substantive Records *See:* PROGRAM RECORDS

Substitution Microfilming *See:* DISPOSAL MICRO-FILMING

SUMMARY GUIDE A GUIDE lacking in detail and DEPTH OF DESCRIPTION, usually prepared to inform potential USERS of the general nature of HOLDINGS. The summary guide usually contains the titles of RECORD GROUPS and MANUSCRIPT GROUPS, SUBGROUPS, and SERIES and their dates and quantity. A summary guide is also known as a summary of records.

SUMMARY INVENTORY An INVENTORY lacking in DEPTH OF DESCRIPTION, usually prepared for material very technical in its FORM (2) and CONTENT, or very homogeneous, or for which little research or reference use is foreseen. Summary inventories are frequently called series or title inventories.

Summary of Records *See:* SUMMARY GUIDE

SURFACE CLEANING The cleaning of DOCUMENTS through the careful use of soft erasers and brushes to remove surface dirt in order to prevent it from becoming embedded in PAPER fibers.

SURVEY 1. A DOCUMENT assembling information relating to specified subject(s) or problem(s) as a basis for planning and decision-making. (ICA) 2. A DOCUMENT resulting from the formal inspection of landed property giving details of its nature, extent, and location, and sometimes used as the basis for tax assessment. (ICA)

Survey, Records *See:* RECORDS SURVEY

Suspense File *See:* TICKLER FILE

SYNDETICS The cross-referencing structure of a CONTROLLED VOCABULARY, which can include such concepts as "USED FOR," "SEE," "SEE ALSO," "BROADER TERM," and "NARROWER TERM" references.

TAB A projection beyond the main body of a guide or FOLDER upon which a caption appears.

Tab Card *See:* PUNCHED CARD/TAPE

Tabulating Card *See:* PUNCHED CARD/TAPE

Tag *See:* FIELD-TAG

Tape Recording *See:* SOUND RECORDING

TARGET A DOCUMENT containing identifying information, coding, or test charts, used in microfilming. Each target constitutes one FRAME.

Teaching Packet *See:* ARCHIVAL TEACHING UNIT

TECHNICAL DRAWING A PLAN, elevation, cross-section, detail, diagram, or MAP made for use in an engineering, architectural, or other technical CONTEXT. (ICA)

TEMPORARY RECORDS In RECORDS MANAGEMENT, RECORDS appraised as having temporary or limited value and approved for DESTRUCTION, either immediately or after a specified RETENTION PERIOD. Temporary records are also called disposable records.

TERMINAL DIGIT FILING A system of numerical filing using the last two or three digits of each number as the primary division under which the RECORD is filed. (ARMA)

TERRITORIAL PERTINENCE The geographical area to which a group of DOCUMENTS pertains. Since World War II, it has been generally agreed that territorial pertinence should give way to TERRITORIAL PROVENANCE as the primary consideration in deciding the destination of archival material when territorial changes occur.

TERRITORIAL PROVENANCE The origin of a group of DOCUMENTS with respect to geographical areas. The concept is directly linked to the principle that archival material should not be removed from the territory in which it was created.

TEXTUAL RECORDS/ARCHIVES RECORDS/ARCHIVES in which the information contained therein is represented as text (written, printed, or displayed words and/or numbers) readable by the eye, even if with the mediation of a machine. *See also:* NONTEXTUAL RECORDS/ARCHIVES

Thematic Guide *See:* GUIDE (2)

THERMOGRAPHY Photocopying processes relying upon heat for formation of the IMAGE. (ICA)

THERMOHYGROMETER A non-recording device used to measure both relative humidity and temperature. *See also:* HYGROTHERMOGRAPH

Thermoplastic Lamination *See:* LAMINATION

THESAURUS A compilation of words and phrases showing synonymous, hierarchical, and other relationships and dependencies, the function of which is to provide a standardized vocabulary for information storage and retrieval. Component parts are an INDEX VOCABULARY and a LEAD-IN VOCABULARY. (ALA) *See also:* AUTHORITY FILE, CONTROLLED VOCABULARY

TICKLER FILE A date-sequenced FILE (2) by which matters pending are flagged for attention on the proper date.

TITLE BLOCK The space on a MAP or architectural/engineering DRAWING set aside for identifying information.

Title Entry *See:* ENTRY

TOTAL ARCHIVES In Canada, ARCHIVES (3) whose responsibilities include RECORDS/ARCHIVES and other materials of research value irrespective of PROVENANCE or type of DOCUMENT.

TRANSACTION An act, or several interconnected acts, in which more than one person is concerned, and by which the relations of such persons between themselves are altered.

Transactional File *See:* CASE FILE

Transactions *See:* PROCEEDINGS

TRANSCRIPT 1. A COPY or REPRODUCTION, in so far as the resources of script and/or typography allow, of an ORIGINAL DOCUMENT, with the exception that abbreviations, if their interpretation is clear, may be extended. (ICA)
2. In legal proceedings, an exact COPY of a text. (ICA)
3. A verbatim written, typed, or printed version of the spoken word, e.g., proceedings in a court of law or an oral history interview. (ICA)

TRANSFER 1. The act involved in a change of physical CUSTODY of RECORDS/ARCHIVES with or without change of legal title. (ICA)
2. RECORDS/ARCHIVES so transferred. (ICA)

TRANSFER CASE/FILE/BOX A container used to transfer DOCUMENTS from one physical location to another, sometimes used for long-term storage. *See also:* ARCHIVES BOX/CONTAINER; RECORDS CENTER CONTAINER/CARTON

TRANSFER LIST A list of RECORDS/ARCHIVES affected by a single TRANSFER. (ICA) *See also:* TRANSMITTAL LIST

Transfer Schedule *See:* RECORDS SCHEDULE

TRANSFERRING AGENCY The AGENCY or organization that transfers a group of RECORDS to a RECORDS CENTER or ARCHIVES (3). It may be the creating or CONTROLLING AGENCY, but need not be. *See also:* CREATOR; OFFICE OF ORIGIN

TRANSMITTAL LIST A DOCUMENT that lists the RECORDS being transferred from a TRANSFERRING AGENCY to a RECORDS CENTER or ARCHIVES (3). The DOCUMENT may also transfer legal responsibility for the RECORDS as well as physical CUSTODY, and may include the physical location in the RECORDS

CENTER or ARCHIVES (2) where the RECORDS are shelved. *See also:* TRANSFER LIST

TRANSPARENCY A photographic IMAGE on transparent material used for viewing or projecting by transmitted light, or for making COPIES. *See also:* SLIDE

Treatment of Correspondence *See:* CORRESPONDENCE MANAGEMENT

TUB FILE An open-top vertical file container normally used for storing high activity RECORDS at their point of use.

TYPESCRIPT A typed DOCUMENT. (ICA) *See also:* MANUSCRIPT

ULTRAFICHE A MICROFICHE with a REDUCTION RATIO greater than 90X. (ICA)

ULTRAVIOLET LAMP A lamp emitting ultraviolet radiation for the examination of faded DOCUMENTS. An ultraviolet lamp is also called a quartz lamp and Wood's lamp. (ICA)

ULTRAVIOLET LIGHT FILTER A screen or sleeve for absorbing ultraviolet radiation from such high ultraviolet radiation sources as sunlight or fluorescent lights.

UNIT OF DESCRIPTION The archival entity (e.g., FONDS, RECORD GROUP, COLLECTION (1,2), SERIES, or ITEM) for which a DESCRIPTIVE RECORD is created.

UNITIZED FILM Roll MICROFILM separated into individual FRAMES or strips and inserted into a MICROFILM JACKET or carrier.

UNSCHEDULED RECORDS RECORDS for which final DISPOSITION has not been determined. *See also:* RECORDS SCHEDULE

UPRIGHT The shelving element which frames the width of the BAY and supports the shelves within the BAY. (ICA)

"USE" REFERENCE A notation under a non-preferred HEADING (2) in an AUTHORITY FILE or THESAURUS that indicates the preferred HEADING (2). *See also:* "USED FOR" REFERENCE

USE/USER STUDY An investigation (qualitative or quantitative) that seeks to identify and understand the demographic and occupational characteristics of USERS of ARCHIVES (3) and MANUSCRIPT REPOSITORIES and their information needs, the physical handling of archival materials, or the

application of archival information to specific types of research or problems. Common data gathering methods include interviews, observation, questionnaires, surveys, and forms analysis.

"USED FOR" REFERENCE A notation under a preferred HEADING (2) in an AUTHORITY FILE or THESAURUS to indicate which non-preferred HEADINGS (2) in the list are cross-referenced to the preferred HEADING (2). *See also:* "USE" REFERENCE

USER Anyone who makes use of information found in archival materials or who uses the services of an ARCHIVES (3) or MANUSCRIPT REPOSITORY. USERS include CREATORS and other ARCHIVISTS as well as RESEARCHERS. *See also:* RESEARCHER

USER EDUCATION The education and training of actual and potential USERS of archival materials in matters such as REFERENCE SERVICE; the availability, use, and interpretation of archival materials; and the value of archival work. *See also:* OUTREACH PROGRAM

USMARC FORMAT A communications FORMAT (3) developed at the Library of Congress for producing and distributing machine-readable bibliographic records on MAGNETIC TAPE. *See also:* USMARC FORMAT FOR ARCHIVAL AND MANUSCRIPTS CONTROL (USMARC AMC)

USMARC FORMAT FOR ARCHIVAL AND MANUSCRIPTS CONTROL (USMARC AMC) A USMARC FORMAT, endorsed by the Society of American Archivists, for the exchange of descriptive and administrative information about archival materials. The FORMAT (3), popularly known as the AMC FORMAT, is jointly administered by the Society of American Archivists and the Library of Congress.

VACUUM DRYING The treatment of water-soaked DOCUMENTS by placing them in a vacuum chamber, creating a vacuum, and introducing warm, dry air. If materials have been previously frozen, most of the water in the ice becomes liquid before changing to the gaseous state, thus making feathering of inks and other water-related problems a possibility. *See also:* VACUUM FREEZE DRYING

VACUUM FREEZE DRYING The treatment of water-soaked DOCUMENTS by freezing to prevent further damage from water in its liquid state, and subsequent drying under high vacuum with the controlled application of heat, usually from heating coils installed in special shelving. The water, in the form of ice, sublimates directly from a solid to a gaseous state. *See also:* VACUUM DRYING

VALUATION The determination, based upon fair market prices, of the monetary value of DOCUMENTS. In Canada, valuation is also known as monetary appraisal.

Vapor Phase Deacidification *See:* DEACIDIFICATION

Variable-Length Field *See:* FIELD

Variable-Occurrence Field *See:* FIELD

VAULT A maximum security storage area constructed of fire-resistant material and structurally independent from the building in which it is located. (ICA)

VELLUM Traditionally, unsplit calfskin, specially treated to be used as a writing MEDIUM and in binding. Vellum may also be made from lambskin or goatskin. Today, the term is sometimes used interchangeably with PARCHMENT.

VERSO The left-hand PAGE of a book or the back of a separate SHEET. *See also:* RECTO

VERTICAL FILE Equipment which stores RECORDS from front to back rather than side to side. (ARMA) *See also:* LATERAL FILE

VERTICAL FILING The storage of DOCUMENTS in an upright position as distinguished from FLAT-FILING. (ICA)

VESICULAR FILM A type of FILM in which EXPOSURE of a light-sensitive component creates vesicles (bubbles) that form a latent IMAGE, made permanent by heating and subsequent cooling. This type of FILM is used for the production of copies from other FILMS; it is not considered to be of ARCHIVAL QUALITY. *See also:* DIAZO FILM; SILVER GELATIN FILM

VIDEODISC An analog OPTICAL DISC used for the storage of video and audio signals. Videodiscs are recorded at the point of manufacture and are read-only devices. *See also:* OPTICAL DISC; COMPACT DISC

VIDEOTAPE A MAGNETIC TAPE on which visual IMAGES are electronically recorded, with or without sound. (ICA) *See also:* MOTION PICTURE

Visual Media *See:* AUDIO-VISUAL RECORDS/ARCHIVES

VITAL RECORD A RECORD containing information essential to re-establish or continue an organization in the event of a disaster. Vital records comprise the RECORDS necessary to re-create the organization's legal and financial status, and to determine the rights and obligations of employees, customers, stockholders, and citizens.

VITAL RECORDS MANAGEMENT The application of RECORDS MANAGEMENT principles and techniques to ensure the preservation of VITAL RECORDS in cases of emergency or after a disaster. *See also:* DISPERSAL; DISASTER PLAN

VITAL RECORDS SCHEDULE Detailed instructions identifying types of VITAL RECORDS, locations, and retention requirements. (ARMA)

VITAL STATISTICS PUBLIC RECORDS of births, marriages, deaths, and disease, kept by a state, city, or other government subdivision under a statutory provision.

VOLUME 1. MANUSCRIPT or printed SHEETS bound together within a cover. (ICA)
2. The physical space occupied by a group of DOCUMENTS.

Waste Book *See:* DAYBOOK

WATERMARK A translucent mark or design in PAPER incorporated during manufacture for purposes of decoration or identification.

WEEDING The removal of individual DOCUMENTS or FILES lacking continuing value from a SERIES. Weeding is also known as culling, purging, or stripping. (ICA) *See also:* SCREENING

WILL The written legal expression or declaration of a person's wishes as to the disposition of his/her property, to be performed or to take effect upon his/her death.

Wood's Lamp *See:* ULTRAVIOLET LAMP

WORD-BY-WORD ARRANGEMENT Arrangement of words and phrases using words rather than letters as filing units. In this system, spaces between words and sometimes marks of punctuation are treated as filing elements. *See also:* LETTER-BY-LETTER ARRANGEMENT

WORKING PAPERS DOCUMENTS, such as DRAFTS, rough NOTES, and calculations, created or assembled and used in the analysis or preparation of other DOCUMENTS. (ICA)

Writ *See:* BRIEF (2)

Xerography *See:* ELECTROSTATIC PROCESS

Appendix

Abbreviations Used by Manuscript Collectors, Curators, and Dealers

The following list is not exhaustive. Rather, the authors have attempted to supply those abbreviations and meanings that are used with some consistency and for which some reliable authority exists. Many, but not all, abbreviations appearing here are also found in the list of abbreviations in *The Manuscript Society Criteria for Describing Manuscripts and Documents*, which is fully cited in the bibliography. The two lists, while not identical in their terms and definitions, are in close conformity. Terms appearing entirely in upper case in this appendix are defined in the main body of this volume.

A, Auto. AUTOGRAPH (2).

AD Autographed DOCUMENT unsigned (an unsigned document in the hand of the author). *See:* D

ADS Autographed DOCUMENT signed (a document, signed and entirely in the hand of the author). *See:* D

AES Autographed ENDORSEMENT signed (an endorsement on another DOCUMENT in the endorser's hand).

AL Autographed LETTER unsigned (an unsigned letter in the hand of the author).

ALS Autographed LETTER signed (a letter, signed and entirely in the hand of the author).

AMs Autographed MANUSCRIPT unsigned (an unsigned manuscript in the hand of the author).

AMsS Autographed MANUSCRIPT signed (a manuscript, signed and entirely in the hand of the author).

AMuD Autographed musical DOCUMENT unsigned (an unsigned musical score, written in the hand of the composer).

AMuDS Autographed musical DOCUMENT signed (a musical score, signed and entirely in the hand of the composer).

AMuQ Autographed musical quotation unsigned (an unsigned excerpt from a musical score, written in the hand of the composer).

AMuQS Autographed musical quotation signed (an excerpt from a musical score, signed and entirely in the hand of the composer).

AN Autographed NOTE unsigned (an unsigned brief, informal LETTER or message, often fragmentary, in the hand of the author).

ANS Autographed NOTE signed (a signed brief, informal LETTER or message, often fragmentary, entirely in the hand of the author).

AQS Autographed quotation signed (a quotation by a person of another's or his/her own words, entirely in the hand of the person doing the quoting).

c., ca. Circa (approximate date).

C. Card (a postcard, picture postcard, or greeting card).

cds Circular date stamp (postal cancellation stamp).

D DOCUMENT. Anything printed, typed, or written, relied upon to record or prove something. Note that this meaning of document (as defined by the Manuscript Society) is narrower than that found in the body of this glossary. Those who use this abbreviation often use it to denote an official record or legal document.

DS DOCUMENT signed (a document, handwritten, not in the hand of the author, but signed by the author). *See:* D

Df DRAFT.

Diagr(s). Diagram(s).

Dup., Dupl. Duplicate.

fac., facs., facsim. FACSIMILE.

FDC First day COVER (postal cover canceled on the first day stamp is issued). First day covers frequently bear souvenir autographs.

Ills., Illus. Illustration or illustrated.

IPS Inscribed PHOTOGRAPH signed (a photograph with dedication and SIGNATURE in hand of the subject).

Jour. JOURNAL.

l, lf, 1 (the letter "l" printed and sometimes in script and also the numeral one). LEAF.

L LETTER. This abbreviated form seldom stands alone and usually is seen in such combinations as AL, ALS, LS.

LS LETTER signed (a letter, handwritten, not in the hand of the author, but signed by the author), e.g., a letter written by a secretary and signed by the author. If typed, the letter should be designated as TLS.

L S, L.S. *Locus sigilli,* Latin for "in place of the SEAL," the place occupied by the seal on written INSTRUMENTS. This abbreviation is often found beside the SIGNATURES of persons on such legal DOCUMENTS instead of, i.e., in place of a seal. The abbreviation does not mean "legal signature."

mem. Memoir.

Ms, MS, mss., MSS MANUSCRIPT; manuscripts. This abbreviation is used as a noun, and is seldom found alone, usually being combined as AMs, etc. The abbreviation has a varied, even vague, meaning, ranging from a literary DOCUMENT prepared for publication to any handwritten or typed DOCUMENT. As an abbreviation, it is often used interchangeably with DOCUMENT.

MsS MANUSCRIPT signed (handwritten, not in the hand of the author, but signed by the author).

MuDS Musical DOCUMENT signed (a musical score, not in the hand of the composer, but signed by the composer).

MuQS Musical quotation signed (an excerpt from a musical score, handwritten, not in the hand of the composer, but signed by the composer).

N NOTE (a brief, informal LETTER or message, often fragmentary). This abbreviated form seldom stands alone and usually is seen in such combinations as AN and ANS.

n.d. No date. This abbreviation in an ENTRY (2) or other DESCRIPTION (2) is used to show that the material itself bears no date. *See also:* n.y.

n.p. No place. This abbreviation is included when there is no indication of the place where the ITEM was written.

n.y. No year, meaning that the day and month may appear, but not the year. *See also:* n.d.

p., pp. PAGE and pages.

pam. Pamphlet.

PS Signed PHOTOGRAPH (a photograph signed in the hand of the subject).

Q Quotation (a quotation by one person of another's words, or of his/her own words). This abbreviation seldom stands alone in a CATALOG, CALENDAR, etc., and is usually found in such combinations as AQS.

rept. REPORT.

S, Sgd. Signed. This abbreviation indicates that the DOCUMENT, LETTER, NOTE, etc. has been personally signed by the author. The abbreviation normally does not stand alone, but is found in such combinations as: ADS, ALS, ANS, AQS, DS, LS, TDS, and TLS.

SFL Stampless folded LETTER. This abbreviation refers to a letter sheet bearing handwritten postal marks without adhesive STAMPS (2).

Sgd. *See:* S, Sgd.

Sig. SIGNATURE.

TDS Typewritten DOCUMENT signed by the author. *See:* D

TLS Typewritten LETTER signed by the author.

TMsS Typewritten MANUSCRIPT signed by the author.

v., vol. VOLUME (2).

Additional Reading

The authors relied on both written sources and discussion with professional peers to develop this glossary. The written sources, most of which are published, are identified below. Some, like this volume, are general glossaries; others are studies of archival concepts and practice; and others are specialized glossaries, thesauri, manuals, or studies. Full citations for sources noted in this essay are found in the bibliography that follows it.

The intellectual forebear of this work is "A Basic Glossary for Archivists, Manuscript Curators, and Records Managers," compiled by Evans et al. and published in 1974 in the *American Archivist*. Like this volume it was based on the work of a committee, the SAA Committee on Terminology, that labored for several years to develop a standard nomenclature. The "Evans Glossary," as the SAA glossary is sometimes called, has remained for years a de facto standard for the Society of American Archivists. Readers are invited to consult it in conjunction with this volume to observe similarities between the two glossaries, as well as changes in terminology since the release of the earlier work.

The SAA basic glossary is one of the written sources most heavily consulted by the authors. Another heavily used source is its international equivalent, the *Dictionary of Archival Terminology,* compiled by Evans et al., published by the International Council on Archives in 1984, and soon to be reissued in revised form. The ICA glossary, another product of a committee, provides terms and definitions in both English and French, and lists equivalent Dutch, German, Italian, Russian, and Spanish terms. The English definitions frequently note North American variations in usage. The authors of this volume have attempted to conform to the ICA glossary except where it did not appear to reflect dominant North American practice.

It is worth noting that there is some continuity in membership on the three glossary projects. Frank B. Evans was a committee member and a compiler for both the SAA and the ICA projects. He was also a committee member for this project. David Horn served on the committees of both SAA glossary projects.

The standard archival literature provides insights on terminology. T. R. Schellenberg's *The Management of Archives* and *Modern Archives: Principles and Techniques* set out classical archival concepts and terminology. So do the essays of Margaret Cross Norton in Thornton Mitchell's edited collection, *Norton on Archives*. A recent general work is Ann Pederson, *Keeping Archives*. Another useful general work is *Understanding Archives and Manuscripts* by James M. O'Toole, one of two manuals in the SAA Archival Fundamentals Series published at the time this glossary was completed. As an introduction to the concepts and principles of archival work, it discusses the changing professional landscape confronting archivists, manuscript curators, and records managers.

The reader interested in terminology might also review other manuals issued by the Society of American Archivists. The Basic Manual Series contains a number of volumes that include information on terminology. So does the new Archival Fundamentals Series. David B. Gracy's *Archives and Manuscripts: Arrangement and Description* in the earlier series and Fredric M. Miller's *Arranging and Describing Archives and Manuscripts* in the Archival Fundamentals Series include many terms used regularly in the processing of archival materials. Margaret Hedstrom's *Archives & Manuscripts: Machine-Readable Records* explains many terms and concepts related to electronic records. Gary M. and Trudy Huskamp Peterson's *Archives and Manuscripts: Law* includes archival terminology relating to such legal issues as access, ownership, and copyright. Three manuals broadly in the area of preservation include Mary Lynn Ritzenthaler's *Archives and Manuscripts: Conservation, a Manual on Physical Care and Management*, Ritzenthaler et al., *Administration of Photographic Collections* in the Basic Manual Series, and Ritzenthaler, *Preserving Archives and Manuscripts* (in preparation) in the Archival Fundamentals Series.

Other works relate to terminology in particular subspecialties. Several focus on archival description. *Anglo-American Cataloguing Rules*, 2nd edition (frequently called *AACR 2*), edited by Michael Gorman and Paul W. Winkler and issued by the American Library Association, is the standard for cataloguing library materials. Steven Hensen's *Archives, Personal Papers, and Manuscripts* (commonly referred to as *APPM*) is the cataloguing standard for archival materials recognized by the Society of American Archivists. The Canadian descriptive standard is *Rules for Archival Description*, issued by the Bureau of Canadian Archivists. All three works include and define terminology relating to bibliographic description. At the time of this writing, the Ad Hoc Commission on Descriptive Standards of the International Council on Archives had prepared a glossary of terms relating to description in its *Statement of Principles Regarding Archival Description*, which is still in draft form.

Additional works focusing on description include Nancy Sahli's *MARC for Archives and Manuscripts: The AMC Format*, which examines and defines fields in the MARC AMC format. This volume was issued by the SAA, which also issued "Understanding the MARC AMC Format Workshop: Glossary" as part of its MARC AMC workshops. *Archival Description Standards*, produced by the Working Group on Standards for Archival Description, provides considerable information relevant to description terminology. It also contains a glossary of acronyms for organizations and standards relating to description.

Related professional associations have published glossaries. The American Library Association has issued the *ALA Glossary of Library and Information Science*. This volume, edited by Heartsill Young, is addressed in particular to librarians, but also covers a wide range of terminology for other information professionals. The Association for Information and Image Management has published *The Glossary of Micrographics*. AIIM is a standards-formulating organization in the area of micrographics, and a number of its definitions are quite technical. The Association of Records Managers and Administrators (ARMA) has issued the *Glossary of Records Management Terms*, which includes a number of indexing and filing terms as well as other records management nomenclature. A committee of the Manuscript Society, in an effort to standardize the description and grading of manuscripts, recently developed *The Manuscript Society Criteria for Describing Manuscripts and Documents*, edited by Norman F. Boas.

The volume contains some definitions and a list of standard abbreviations for manuscripts. The National Association of Government Archives and Records Administrators (NAGARA) has worked for a number of years to develop standard reporting criteria for government archives, especially state archives. A product of this work is *Program Reporting Guidelines for Government Records Programs*, which contains a number of terms and definitions.

Because documents are fundamental to the work of records managers, manuscript curators, and archivists, definitions of document types are valuable, especially to entering professionals. *Black's Law Dictionary* contains a surprising number of definitions of document types. It also supplements the Peterson et al. volume cited above for concepts and principles relating to archives and the law. Edwin A. Thompson's "A Glossary of American Historical and Literary Manuscript Terms" defines many document types. Lastly, the *Art and Architecture Thesaurus*, which was developed as a project of the J. Paul Getty Trust, contains a large document type hierarchy with definitions. The *AAT*, edited under the direction of Toni Petersen, is available both in print and on-line. Where possible, the authors have attempted to be congruent with the *AAT* document type terminology.

Diplomatics is a field not yet widely taught in North America. However, its concepts and terminology are important for archival work. Luciana Duranti's article, "Diplomatics: New Uses for an Old Science," provides an introduction to this field.

A fuller list of sources used by the authors in compiling this glossary follows:

The American Heritage Dictionary, Second College Edition. Boston: Houghton Mifflin Company, 1982.

Association for Information and Image Management. *Glossary of Micrographics: AIIM TR2-1980*. Silver Spring, Maryland: AIIM, 1980.

Association of Records Managers and Administrators, Inc. *Glossary of Records Management Terms*. Prairie Village, Kansas: ARMA, 1985.

Bearman, David. *Optical Media: Their Implications for Archives and Museums*. Archival Informatics Technical Report, vol. 1, no. 1, Spring, 1987.

Black, Henry Campbell. *Black's Law Dictionary: Definitions of the Terms and Phrases of American and English Jurisprudence, Ancient and*

Modern, 5th ed. St. Paul, Minnesota: West Publishing Co., 1979.

Boas, Norman F., ed. *The Manuscript Society Criteria for Describing Manuscripts and Documents*. Burbank, California: The Manuscript Society, 1990.

Bowers, Fredson Thayer. *Principles of Bibliographic Description*. New York: Russell & Russell, 1962.

Bureau of Canadian Archivists, Planning Committee on Descriptive Standards. *Rules for Archival Description*. Ottawa: Bureau of Canadian Archivists, 1990.

Carter, John. *ABC for Book Collectors*, 5th ed., revised. New York: Knopf, 1988.

Cook, Michael. *Archives and the Computer*. London: Butterworths, 1980.

Couture, Carol and Jean-Yves Rousseau. *The Life of A Document: A Global Approach to Archives and Records Management*. Translated by David Homel. Montreal: Vehicule Press, 1987.

Duckett, Kenneth W. *Modern Manuscripts: A Practical Manual for their Management, Care, and Use*. Nashville, Tennessee: American Association for State and Local History, [1975].

Duranti, Luciana. "Diplomatics: New Uses for an Old Science." *Archivaria* 28 (Summer 1989): 7–27.

Evans, Frank B., Francois-J. Himly, and Peter Walne, comps.; and Peter Walne, ed. *Dictionary of Archival Terminology*, ICA Handbooks Series, vol. 3. New York, London, Paris: K. G. Saur Munchen, 1984.

Evans, Frank B., Donald F. Harrison, and Edwin A. Thompson, comps.; and William L. Rofes, ed. "A Basic Glossary for Archivists, Manuscript Curators, and Records Managers." *American Archivist* 37 (July 1974): 415-433.

Evans, Henry Herman, comp. *A Guide to Rare Books*. San Francisco: Porpoise Bookshop, 1948.

Fischer, Barbara. "Terms Used in Archival Repositories, Historical Societies, and Library Manuscript Collections," in draft manual by Fischer in possession of Frank B. Evans.

Glaister, Geoffrey Ashall. *Glossary of the Book*. Berkeley: University of California Press, 1979.

Gorman, Michael and Paul W. Winkler, eds. *Anglo-American Cataloguing Rules*. 2nd ed., revised. Chicago: American Library Association, 1988.

Gracy, David B. *Archives and Manuscripts: Arrangement and Description*. SAA Basic Manual Series. Chicago: Society of American Archivists, 1977.

Gracy, David B. "Archivists, You are What People Think You Keep." *American Archivist* 52 (Winter 1989): 72–78.

Gunn, Michael J. *Manual of Document Microphotography*. London and Boston: Focal Press, 1985.

Gwinn, Nancy E., ed. *Preservation Microfilming: A Guide for Librarians and Archivists*. Chicago and London: American Library Association, 1987.

Haller, Margaret. *The Book Collector's Fact Book*. New York: Arco Publishing Co., 1976.

Ham, F. Gerald. *Selecting and Appraising Archives and Manuscripts*. Archival Fundamentals Series. Chicago: Society of American Archivists, forthcoming.

Harrod's Librarians' Glossary of Terms Used in Librarianship, Documentation, and the Book Crafts and Reference Book, 5th ed., revised and updated by Ray Prytherch; Leonard Montague Harrod, advisory editor. Brookfield, Vermont: Gower Publishing Company, 1984.

Hedstrom, Margaret L. *Archives & Manuscripts: Machine-Readable Records*. SAA Basic Manual Series. Chicago: Society of American Archivists, 1984.

Hensen, Steven. *Archives, Personal Papers, and Manuscripts: A Cataloging Manual for Archival Repositories, Historical Societies, and Manuscript Libraries*, 2nd ed. Chicago: Society of American Archivists, 1989.

Hickerson, H. Thomas. *Archives and Manuscripts: An Introduction to Automated Access*. SAA Basic Manual Series. Chicago: Society of American Archivists, 1981.

International Council on Archives, Ad Hoc Commission on Descriptive Standards. *Statement of Principles Regarding Archival Description*, draft. Ottawa: ICA, 1990.

Lewis, Alan F. Letter to Lewis Bellardo, April 21, 1988.

Maedke, Wilmer O., Mary F. Robek, and Gerald F. Brown. *Information and Records Management.* 3rd ed. Mission Hills, California: Glencoe McGraw Hill, 1987.

Miller, Fredric M. *Arranging and Describing Archives and Manuscripts.* Archival Fundamentals Series. Chicago: Society of American Archivists, 1990.

National Archives and Records Administration, Office of Records Administration, Agency Services Division. *A Federal Records Management Glossary.* [Washington]: National Archives and Records Administration, 1989.

National Archives and Records Service. *The Preparation of Inventories*, Staff Information Paper 14. Washington: National Archives and Records Service, 1976.

National Association of Government Archives and Records Administrators. *Program Reporting Guidelines for Government Records Programs.* n.p.: National Association of Government Archives and Records Administrators and the Council of State Governments, n.d.

Norton, Margaret Cross. *Norton on Archives: The Writings of Margaret Cross Norton on Archival & Records Management.* Edited by Thornton Mitchell. Chicago: Society of American Archivists, 1979.

O'Toole, James M. *Understanding Archives and Manuscripts.* Archival Fundamentals Series. Chicago: Society of American Archivists, 1990.

Pederson, Ann, editor-in-chief. *Keeping Archives.* Sydney, Australia: Australian Society of Archives, Incorporated, 1987.

Peters, Jean, ed. *The Bookman's Glossary*, 6th ed., revised and enlarged. New York and London: R. R. Bowker Company, 1986.

Petersen, Toni, ed. *Art & Architecture Thesaurus.* New York: Oxford University Press for the J. Paul Getty Trust, 1990.

Peterson, Gary M. and Trudy Huskamp Peterson. *Archives and Manuscripts: Law.* SAA Basic Manual Series. Chicago: Society of American Archivists, 1985.

Pugh, Mary Jo. *Providing Reference Services for Archives and Manuscripts.* Archival Fundamen-

tals Series. Chicago: Society of American Archivists, forthcoming.

Ritzenthaler, Mary Lynn. *Archives and Manuscripts: Conservation, a Manual on Physical Care and Management.* SAA Basic Manual Series. Chicago: Society of American Archivists, 1983.

Ritzenthaler, Mary Lynn. *Preserving Archives and Manuscripts.* Archival Fundamentals Series. Chicago: Society of American Archivists, forthcoming.

Ritzenthaler, Mary Lynn, Gerald J. Munoff, and Margery S. Long. *Administration of Photographic Collections.* SAA Basic Manual Series. Chicago: Society of American Archivists, 1984.

Roberts, Matt T. and Don Etherington. *Bookbinding and the Conservation of Books: A Dictionary of Descriptive Terminology.* Washington: Library of Congress, 1982.

Sahli, Nancy. *MARC for Archives and Manuscripts: The AMC Format.* Chicago: Society of American Archivists, 1985.

Schellenberg, T. R. *The Management of Archives.* New York: Columbia University Press, 1963.

Schellenberg, T. R. *Modern Archives: Principles and Techniques.* Chicago: University of Chicago Press, 1956.

Society of American Archivists. "Understanding the MARC AMC Format Workshop: Glossary." Chicago: Society of American Archivists, n.d.

Society of American Archivists, Committee on Finding Aids. *Inventories and Registers: A Handbook of Techniques and Examples, a Report of the Committee on Finding Aids.* Chicago: Society of American Archivists, 1976.

Society of American Archivists, Committee on Goals and Priorities. *An Action Agenda for the Archival Profession: Institutionalizing the Planning Process.* [Chicago]: Society of American Archivists, 1988.

Thompson, Edwin A., comp. "A Glossary of American Historical and Literary Manuscript Terms," unpublished manuscript, 1965. National Archives Library, Washington.

United Nations. *Management of Electronic Records: Issues and Guidelines.* New York: United Nations, 1990.

Wilsted, Thomas and William Nolte. *Managing Archival and Manuscript Repositories*. Archival Fundamentals Series. Chicago: Society of American Archivists, 1991.

Working Group on Standards for Archival Description. *Archival Description Standards: Establishing a Process for Their Development and Implementation, Report and Recommendations of the Working Group on Standards for Archival Description*. Prepublication copy, 1990. Also published in the *American Archivist* 52 (Fall 1989): 430–537; and 53 (Winter 1990): 24–108.

Yates, JoAnne. *Control through Communication: The Rise of System in American Management*. Baltimore: Johns Hopkins University Press, 1989.

Young, Heartsill, ed. *The ALA Glossary of Library and Information Science*. Chicago: American Library Association, 1983.